Relentless

DAVEY ASHFIELD

APS Books
Yorkshire

APS Books

APS Books is a subsidiary of the APS Publications imprint

www.andrewsparke.com

Cover art by Gwyneth Hibbett

First published worldwide by APS Books in 2021

A catalogue record for this book is available from the British Library

ISBN 978-1-78996-437-0

For Eddy
And his beloved sister

And
Les, Nev, Steve, Pete, Keith old and new, Kevin, Jacqui and
our poor bairns
& all the others who stood with me through it all

Keep the Faith

CONTENTS

RELENTLESS MISERY

'Did ah tell yeah Mick what my last bucket list thing was?'

Mick turned to look at the good friend who had sat next to him for many years at Newcastle United's football ground, St James Park. He smiled kindly at the ageing man as they reunited yet again for the first game of the new season. After a few minutes of general chat the man revealed that as he was getting on in years and not in great health he had spent the football close season beginning his last wish *bucket list* items with his loving family. He told Mick of the great things he'd seen and done, thoroughly enjoying being back in each other's company again. But now the game had kicked off and they were watching a particularly dull and uninspiring first match of the season and both were thinking, *Here we go again.* Despite all the hype, close season transfer signings and pre-season game positives, on the park nothing much had changed. So bored and uninterested in what was happening on the pitch the old man turned to Mick and asked him: 'Did ah tell yeah, Mick, what my last bucket list thing was?'

Mick answered his friend's question: 'Nor, yeah didn't. I hope it's a good 'un mate.'

'Aye, it's the one thing I've always wanted to see before I die.'

Mick looked sympathetically at his fellow lifelong supporter. He had recently been very ill himself and now faced an uncertain future so he was curious to learn what was so important enough to be his friend's last wish. 'What's that mate?'

The man's gloomy, despondent voice never faltered as he told of his last hope: 'Ah'd lerv to see Newcastle win a trophy afor I die.'

Mick smiled. *Yup, that's a good one. I'd put that first on mine too.* He looked into his friend's eyes and saw the pain, not of a tired body and mind, but from sixty years of watching his beloved football team without a serious trophy win. Mick could only nod his head in a shared pain. For a second or two the older man stared at Mick dolefully. Then, with a shrug of his shoulders, he dropped his head and turned his gaze back to the field of play. With a dark North

East humour that belied his mortality and pain, he concluded his last bucket list wish. He stared into eternity, muttering assuredly to himself: 'But neebody lives that lang.'

'I am so sorry to tell you but you have cancer'

Marc looked at his doctor in shock, aghast.' That's just my bloody luck,' he exclaimed.

She came around her desk and took his hand to comfort him, saying: 'That's ok. Most people think that. It's a phase of acceptance of the cancer - anger and then denial.'

Marc looked into her caring, compassionate eyes with a look of puzzlement and explained: 'How man, it's not the cancer that's upsetting me. It's just my bloody luck, Sunderland is getting taken over. Ashley has buggered up those black and white bastards yet again with their Arab takeover and now we're going to be richer than them, or Man City, and you tell me I'll not live to see us win the European Cup!'

The doctor shook her head and smiled, acknowledging that in the North East, football madness trumped fear of death. 'Yes, I understand. I studied at Newcastle Medical School. You're all a bit touched aren't you?'

Marc is still surviving the big C but after sixty years supporting them, as I write, he has yet to see Sunderland with more money than Man City or getting out of the third division, never mind a European Championship. He has had the doubtful joy with millions of worldwide viewers on Netflix over two seasons of watching them plummet from the Championship, lose two Wembley finals and fail to be promoted from Division One – *'Sunderland Till I Die'*...the title is becoming prophetic.

'Stop playing that Jacobean shite!'

Harry shouted his anger over the sound of the flute and the large Aberdonian Rangers fan playing, *Flower of Scotland*. The flute player immediately stopped and apologised profusely to the much smaller, older and grizzled Harry and started playing the dulcet notes of *The Sash*. Jack was in the Singapore bar that Harry owned,

The Sportsman's, which was the meeting point of the South East Asia Glasgow Rangers Society. He was standing next to Harry drinking with the patriarch. Curious as always about bizarre human behaviour he asked, 'What's up Harry? I thought it was your National Anthem.'

'It's nae oor National Anthem. It's a Fenian song,' the stocky old Glaswegian growled through his pursed blue lips and he pointed up to the numerous Union Jack flags and the huge picture of the Queen which hung over the bar. 'That's oor flag and that's oor Queen and oor National Anthem is God Save the Queen.'

'Oh,' Jack muttered, still trying to come to terms with quaint Scottish folk songs and schizophrenic patriotism.

'Bonnie Prince Charlie was a Fenian, living in Papist Rome. Jacobite bastard, and ah'll nae have that song in here son,' Harry snarled, his voice as cold as a Clydeside winter. Jack felt it was not the place and time to suggest that *Flower of Scotland* was about Robert the Bruce, a French speaking, Catholic born Scottish King who defeated the English at Bannockburn and not Bonnie Charlie. Scottish history was complicated and Harry's bigoted versions were taken as gospel by all who worshipped in his temple. Jack decided it might be safer to move on to football, but then made a real cultural faux pas.

'Danny is a Partick Thistle fan and he isn't keen on the Queen but won't sing *Flower of Scotland*. What does that make him?'

'For ****'s sake anyone who comes in here and says he's a Thistle fan is a Fenian. They're Celtic. I won't serve the bastards. Celtic's flag is the Irish tricolour and they're Scottish. Oor Flag is the Union Jack and we're British. It's simple really big man.'

Jack studied the scowling, acerbic and miserable man and wondered how on earth football could be so complicated. Harry didn't enjoy any of the actual games on his television screens. He was forever frowning and trying to spot Fenians in his bar and then avoiding serving them to bother with the intricacies of a beautifully taken free kick or a wonder save. Misery seemed to follow him. Jack looked up at the framed photographs of past managers of Rangers that Harry revered. Not one of them had a smile. He shuddered at the photograph of Bill Struth who reminded him of Colonel Cathcart in *Catch 22* and also his old headmaster, Mr Curtis, who could terrify anyone with his glower. All of them looked as if the world of football and its intense rivalry in that divided city had made them medically ill.

And indeed for many in the bar it had.

'I'm being scheduled for a major operation next Saturday'

'You cannae dee that big man. Cancel it. The Jags' match against Forfar is on the Club's online stream,' said Denis to his mate on the *WhatsApp* video call after a few cyber beers in their virtual pub, *The Covid Arms*.

'Aye that's why I told the surgeon I'd be ok that day. I'd rather have a six hour operation than watch that shite.'

And he did

And to continue the Caledonian misery…

'We're shite'

…an angelic small boy dressed in his brand new strip and tartan army scarf said to the BBC Scotland TV reporter as he left Hampden Park holding his father's hand. Then scowling at the reporter he wailed about his beloved national team's strikers: 'They cuddnae finish their ******* dinnas.'

Sadly, the small child had witnessed his first misery of the beautiful game, the defeat by The Czech Republic after his country lost 2-0 in their first match in a major tournament in twenty-two years. With massive patriotism and a whole nation's anticipation of finally winning a trophy on her shoulders, Wee Nicola had let the children who could not attend the match due to social distancing rules watch it at school. One Head Teacher, Wendy Cameron of Broomhill Primary in the West End of Glasgow, with her obvious lack of Scottish football knowledge and with a simple naivety, had declared: 'Maths worksheets and workbooks won't create memories as good as watching the match.'

Well, indeed she may have been correct. The memory of the latest Scottish goalkeeping disaster when the keeper went walkabout and got entangled in the net like an Abroath Smokie might well last in the poor child's memory another twenty-two years before the next tournament and much longer than my old maths' problems question, 'How many men does it take to dig a hole six feet deep and three foot wide?'

But there is always some hope because they play the Auld Enemy next Friday for the first time in a quarter century...like the headmistress, the outrageously biased English media really should learn from history. Football may well be coming home and we may well eat that Vindaloo in Waterloo if you believe the endless media hype. However, after 55 years of disappointments I fear another penalty shoot-out misery coming on and a nationwide huge hangover the next day. Like all the other new Jerusalems we have built on the shifting sands of English hope ,I hope this one ends the fifty-five years of hurt.

I wonder how that one turned out?

'Dad, it's a Relentless Misery'

Ben phoned his father on the landline on the evening of the Saturday 22nd June 2020 because he couldn't get him on his mobile. He was worried for his father because Exeter had lost yet another Third Division play off promotion final at Wembley. It was the third time in four years they'd failed. In the four visits to Wembley he'd made he'd never seen them win. Years of up and down between the Fourth Division, non–league and Third Division and the latest Wembley defeat was the last straw. His dad had smashed his phone off the wooden bar in the mad Irish bar he was drinking in and walked home head in hands yet again. Ben consoled his distraught, manically depressed parent as only a fellow sufferer could with a positive thought: 'I told you Dad – it is a Relentless Misery supporting us.'

And when I heard that story, I thought what a good title it would make for my book on real football supporters who have suffered for so long and began writing. It was particularly applicable to North East supporters who never seem to get a break. *But soft! What light through yonder window breaks?* Unbelievably, as I nearly complete this masterpiece, a Juliette, or less romantically, a miracle Romeo cure for Marc and thousands of Sunderland supporters' mental agony has appeared from the East in the form of a new post-adolescent French owner. Young Mr Dreyfus potentially has enough money to get them to that Champion's League final that Marc might survive long enough to attend...and maybe win that trophy at last. And then as I am about to go into hospital for a serious operation, Sunderland get to Wembley yet again in the Papa John's Trophy (I know...I know, it's a bloody pizza cup and not the Champions League but it's a possible first Wembley win in eight successive finals so it is something to cheer up thousands of tormented Red and White supporters) and as I write they are also looking odds on for a promotion playoff place if not an automatic one. I wonder how all that turns out?

Therefore, as a result of this new found optimism for supporters, well Sunderland football club anyway, and with the optimistic hope I might actually survive the tender mercies of the surgeons, I have asked my offspring to use their IT skills while I am under the knife to change my title, to strike out MISERY and replace it with HOPE. Because, really that's why we all go to football and suffer the relentless misery: *It is the HOPE we can't stand*

So, *'Relentless Misery/Hope'* is a book for supporters from any football club who have travelled to watch football.

It is about Mick's long suffering Newcastle-supporting mate who can make you smile through the pain of yet another defeat with such black humour.

It's definitely yet another gastric ulcer bursting defeat for Manic Marc and a long journey from Portsmouth, Exeter or Gillingham whilst sitting in a minivan jammed with bodies with someone like Ginger Gus sitting on your lap and you can't escape as he farts continually onto your knee, poisoning you slowly.

Possibly, it's about Harry relentlessly worrying about his rival's supporters and the street they were born in, the school they attended and the folk songs they sing rather than the football.

Or maybe it is Ben's dad's hell of yet another Wembley defeat; falling asleep on the train after the match and ending up in a place where they speak a foreign language and eat scones with the jam added first before the cream with no train home for two days.

Without doubt it's Denis's friend who would rather submit to hours of surgical pain than watch a Scottish League One match in mid-February.

Or it's my angst at my fiancé leaving me because her precious new shoes are flooded with gallons of pee flowing down from the terraces above her. And then it is her worst nightmare – the weasel looking Charva standing next to her with his hand stuffed down his stained polyester track suit bottoms playing constantly with his semi-erection, who then, smiling sexily through his brown, nicotine-stained teeth, winks at her amorously.

Or perhaps it's all about an eventful away trip with Crazy Jim, inclusive of fire extinguishers, guns, blind dogs, kidnapping, wheelchairs, and a short time in solitary.

And really folks, it's all these experiences, this collective schadenfreude that makes football supporters keep travelling in their thousands to each others' towns, turning up full of optimism and vainly hoping that one day, just one day, they will avoid another relegation, or get promotion and finally win that trophy.

CHAPTER ONE
North East Doldrums

Manic Marc had lived through ten relegations and nine promotions and God only knows how many near misses either way since he could remember watching his first Sunderland game, which was the Boxing Day match at Roker Park when Brian Clough's playing career was ended. I haven't got the pedantry or the patience to check on the cyber media if Sunderland AFC has the doubtful trophy for the team most relegated and promoted or near misses, but I'd bet a cup of steaming hot Bovril and a lukewarm, grizzle-filled meat pie that they're not far off it. And just to rub it in, Marc has been to Wembley eight times to see them fail to win a game since the one real trophy win in his lifetime, the 1973 FA Cup. And now as I edit this story, Sunderland did indeed win the 2021 Pizza Cup at Wembley but of course to compound the misery Manic Marc and thousands more couldn't finally enjoy a weekend in London and Wembley trip with a happy ending because of a once in a lifetime global pandemic. You couldn't make it up, could you?

Mick and his fellow Newcastle fans haven't experienced so much angst, particularly the agony of the almost annual end of season near misses that Sunderland have experienced, but they have had a penance to pay over the years which belies their position promoted by many as a 'super club'. It is 63 years since they won any blue ribbon domestic honour and have been relegated five and promoted five times since Mick and his friend started watching football. Seven long trips there and back to Wembley and no trophy. And this is after nearly fifty years of being unbeaten there by the time Jackie Milburn scored in the last trophy win for The Magpies in 1955.

Prior to Marc opening this history with the Brian Clough Sunderland v Bury game in 1962, Sunderland had won six first division league titles and one FA cup and Newcastle had won four league titles and six FA cups. Both were regarded as two of the top five teams in the country. Sunderland had once been termed the *Bank of England Club* in the fifties for its ability to attract and pay the best players in the UK. Much good did it do them: they were relegated for the first time in their history in 1958.

Newcastle have at least experienced heady days on top of the Premiership for a brief moment and playing regularly in Europe to huge crowds with exciting world class players. But, despite these heady days, the experience of late has been depressing for everyone. As with Mick's elderly friend's angst, I'm sure all of their supporters would, 'lerve teh win a trophy'. But how long can one man live!

Middlesbrough are the only club to have won anything in most people's lifetime in the North East Region; The League Cup in 2004. This remains the only trophy that Middleborough people have seen their team win in 120 years. I have no idea how many relegations and promotions the supporters of *The Boro'* have had to suffer but I would guess it's not far off both of the other North East teams. Because I'm fond of Harry Pearson's writing and his love of the North East Region's football history, and the fact I know so many crazed sociopathic Boro fans, I'll be kinder than most of my fellow supporters and not mention that Middlesbrough really is in Yorkshire and not strictly what we would call the North East up here. And you really can't have one of your legs in Yorkshire, one leg in Cleveland and one leg in County Durham can you?

Sadly, Hartlepool supporters have, like the monkey they so cruelly hanged all those years ago, been left swinging for too long. And Darlington, well, they were cracked open like too many of the past Chairman's safes he used to gelly and ran off the railways that they did so much to invent.

Nope: it has not been great times for supporters up in the North East this last Century or two. And I guess for supporters of many teams in their own way times have been hard. But don't get me on about Arsenal, Man United and Liverpool supporters whining on about how bad they'd had it. Deaf ears I'm afraid. Read back the couple of pages I've just written and then tell me you've had it bad.

It's the black humour and angst that follows around the supporters of many of our football teams and the comradeship and crazy antics are what keeps most of us going; it's never the actual football. Not for the teams in the North East of England it isn't. And that's where this story is based, only because it is my birthplace and I have stories to tell which I believe will appeal to all supporters.

This is not a *hooligan* book with stories of *git hard* top lads, diamond geezers or *my firm was harder than your firm* - nor is it a mass of statistics, crowd figures or trophies won. Instead it's a collection of funny and cathartic stories of *normal* supporters suffering a roller coaster of thrills and terrors through five decades of the beautiful game. It's about the times spent with parents and grandparents, children and good friends that we have been blessed to know and as Manic Marc always tells anyone who questions why we would put ourselves and loved ones through this - 'It's character building.'

So, here we are. I hope you like them, even if you don't watch football and have had to suffer your kids, friends or partner's misery all these years. Please read it - at least you might understand why they're so demented. Because whoever you support I'm sure you will have suffered greatly but will still have thoroughly enjoyed the magic carpet ride as much as me.

CHAPTER TWO
Leeds, 'Jormans' and Gaddafi

Manic Marc was standing behind the goal in his usual place with several of his mates. They came every week to the match after meeting at the same pub for many years. As usual they had drunk many beers to help quell the agony of watching the team. It was a winter's night and a bitter wind and mist drifted in over the top of the other stand, freezing the travelling fans to a state of hyperthermia. Manic Marc chuckled to himself as he watched the opposition fans freeze because Leeds supporters had a penchant in those days for stripping off to the waist in all weathers and waving their shirts and abdomens around aggressively at the opposing fans to prove how hard they were. A bit like rutting stags, snorting and bellowing and sticking out a hairy chest. At Marc's place of worship they lasted about one song and the shirts were back on.

Marc suspected Roker Park was the coldest ground in the UK - well apart from Pittodrie, Aberdeen's ground, where the ground matched the people - cold, miserable and unfriendly.

Marc still had the newspaper clipping in support of his thoughts on Aberdeen in his wallet. He kept this along with his favourite cuttings that proved his team's crowds had been were far superior to his rivals during Queen Victoria's reign. He smiled, took the cutting out, looked at it and happy in his mania, he put it back in.

> Finally. The Mirror sent reporter Jenny Johnston to Aberdeen to test the claim, made in the British Journal of Psychiatry, that Aberdeen is the nation's most miserable city, where up to 20% of residents suffer from seasonal affective disorder (SAD).
>
> One of the people she approached was a grey-coated man waiting for a bus. Did he think. she asked. that Aberdeen deserved its title as the most miserable place on earth? "F*** off," he replied.

He smiled again when he realised that as usual they had missed the kick off because of the drinking. Young Keith had pushed behind three men standing in front of the barrier that they always stood in front of, rapidly followed by Ginger Gus, Marc, Daft Billy, John, Stan, Paul and Crazy Jim, Young Keith and the kids telling the three new men - 'Out the way and let the real supporters in.' Marc recalled with a grin the excellent book that Harry Pearson wrote, *The Far Corner* and the events when Harry attended the Boxing Day match at Sunderland in 1992. Harry and his mate had been pushed out the way at about exactly the same spot by late coming *real supporters*. These, Harry observed, had consisted of a wiry, mischievous one with ginger hair and 'tash, a huge wax-jacketed one who called out to fellow whales mating off Roker Pier, a long tall beanpole who seemed not at all there in his mental state. Marc was pretty sure it had been him and his friends that Harry had described. He thought, *Mr Pearson, I apologise if it was us. But as you have made many people laugh or cry over these and many other antics and earned a bob or two I can't be too penitent about it. And of course you are a Middlesbrough supporter which means you may have seen these events erringly through your third eye.*

The drink before the game was needed because as usual the match was dire. As a consequence the ground was silent as a graveyard. People were rubbing their hands and stamping their feet to keep warm and staring onto the barren, featureless wilderness of a playing field devoid of entertainment. Many were checking their watches. Marc's mate Keith nudged his friend and suggested: 'This is shite. Let's tilt and get an early pint.'

Marc was about to agree when from a few rows behind a voice began crying out in the wilderness, booming across the whole crowd: 'For God's's sake! Arl ah iver wanted from life was a good football team and a widower's pension. And ah've got nen of the buggers!'

The crowd burst into merriment at the Fulwell End John the Baptist's marital and sports angst. For a while they began another cheer and chant, but it was soon to be replaced by a deep-felt groan at yet another long ball going over the head of the new super European, German striker, Thomas Hauser. His uninterested jump meant he never left the ground by more than a few inches. Then, through the gloom and depressive silence, after the groans had quieted, the same voice was crying out again in the wilderness: 'Dear God man! He rose like the Hindenburg.'

This prophet wasn't a herald predicting the coming of someone who's pit boot laces he wasn't fit to tie but a surrogate Middle

Eastern icon of the time. He was called Gaddafi. He was a tall, blond-haired, bearded and well-built pitman from the Durham village of Hetton-le-Hole. Manic Marc had named him after the Libyan Arab terrorist leader Gaddafi - well one man's terrorist is another man's President. This was because he always wore one of his mother's red and white checked table cloths as a scarf around his neck in the Yasser Arafat style of the day. He stood about a couple of people behind Marc and his mates and his usual acerbic wit cheered them all up during most matches as the beer wore off. The torture and mind numbing boredom of watching matches on days like today's tore into the very soul.

'At last! That useless twat has seen the light...get that lazy Kraut off the park!' shouted Ginger Gus at the manager who was gesturing wildly at his record signing German Zeppelin many yards away on the touchline. He grabbed Marc's arm, swaying slightly, still mortal drunk and then fell into the old man and his son on the next step and through his whispery ginger moustache slurred: 'Ah think he's bringing on the new lad, Marc?'

'Let's hope so. This Jorman is as much use as our lass.'

And to the joy of everyone, to a huge round of applause for the new player and a torrent of abuse at the departing Teutonic gas bag, the new player,bought for a not inconsiderable sum of money because he was supposed to be lightning fast, sprinted on the pitch.

'Give the ball to the new lad, man,' shouted the majority of the crowd to the bandy legged psychopath of a midfield general who had snapped the opposition's winger's leg and taken the ball off him.

'That twat couldn't pass wind man. He's ******** gash,' shouted a blue-rinsed, middle-aged, chubby woman who looked like she should have been in church.

The psychopath must have liked this kind of reverse psychology because for the first time in many a game he curved the ball cunningly around the fullback for the super-fast Usain Bolt look-alike to run onto. The crowd cheered and roared in anticipation of their new signing skinning the opposition fullback only for the noise to collapse into a collective groan as he struggled to outrun the opposition player and then tripped up in a tangle of his own arms and legs off the pitch and onto the surrounding hard core track. The stunned crowd went deathly silent, their delight and anticipation of a super signing once more blown away. Gaddafi's voice boomed over the silence from his minaret as if calling the faithful to prayer: 'For God's sake. We might as well have brought a wardrobe on.'

Some of the crowd around Marc and his mates laughed. Others cried and some just took one more sip of their tepid Bovril and shrugged their shoulders. They'd seen it all before.

Five minutes later the team was awarded a corner and the new superstar came for the first time to the Fulwell End where Marc and his friends were standing. He came close to the crowd and to the corner flag it and Ginger Gus, in his own inimitable way, thought to give him a warm welcome to the zoo where they spent far too much of their precious lives. He leaned forward, howling through his beer-stained ginger moustache, pushing and sticking his head past the blue-rinsed Evangelist lady and her family and drooling on her nicely tailored coat.

'How lad! Yeah'd run a lot faster if yeah'd tak that video player from under yeah arm.'

Quite a few laughed but most just shook their mind-numbed heads. The player looked up from placing the ball and scanned the crowd menacingly. He dropped his head seeing no sympathy at all for his plight. *Welcome to the pleasure dome* he must have thought. He took the corner and watched as the ball sailed hopelessly over the assembled players in the box and out of play on the far side of the pitch. The crowd groaned and the referee blew for time. The new star player, still a tad upset at the video reference, stared into the faceless crowd looking for his tormentor. Ginger Gus, totally uninterested in the man's feelings, had already given up and left in search of a pint. The new signing strode off the pitch, cursing the press yet again for revealing that in his youth he had been a somewhat naughty boy who had brushed with Her Majesty's finest men in blue and so condemning him to exile in the frozen wastes of the North-East of England.

In the pub afterwards the lads talked about the match and all the latest round of new signings who had failed to move them up the table. The nil-nil draw had dropped the team two more places and soon they would have to travel to their rivals for their next game, a promotion derby. No one was feeling very confident. Marc's mate whom he'd coerced into following him into this vale of tears drove him and his two kids the thirty-five miles back to where he now lived. His family had never had any choice of who they supported...it was a birthright, ordained and Newtonian - fixed in time.

It was character building.

CHAPTER THREE
Derby Day, Blind Dogs & Guns and Sheffield

Manic Marc had a traumatic childhood due to the fact that his father and three uncles had been supporters of his rival team. He never spoke for five years which his adoring sister, who also refused to follow her father's team, put down to the horror of having a father who supported *those up the road* and therefore why would her brother want to talk to him anyway. Indeed, sixteen years later when his father died, he wouldn't go to the funeral because his Newcastle-supporting uncles would be there. Having no fatherly guidance or indeed, love - how could he if his dad was one of them - he went alone to the matches with fellow kids from the town and at a very early age travelled and supported the team all over Britain.

His trauma reached new levels when he realised that his mother's cousin's father had played for Newcastle! His name was Jimmy Hagen and he had also played for England. He went on to manage Benfica and Sporting Lisbon in Portugal. Eusébio was one of my favourite players. Who can forget the 1966 World Cup matches in the North East and North West and his goals – a magic player. And he was one of the pall-bearers at Jimmy's funeral. Jimmy had given Marc's mother a photograph signed by the Charlton brothers together as a brotherly pair on the Wembley field at the end of England's World Cup win in 1966. Marc retains this and believes it's the only signed photograph of the two brothers together after the match. He also still remains convinced Bobby was a Sunderland supporter.

Another relation played for a well-known London team and was called *Killer* as he was quite touched in a neuropathic sense and manic in his approach to the game given his dislike of the other players' legs. And as Manic Marc has similar traits, maybe Dawkins is correct. Genes are bastards, and the craziest win through.

Marc was given a box on his beloved Nana's death which contained old heirlooms and photographs and information about his relatives...even the black and white ones. His grandfather's first club card wallet still had his CIU cards in the pocket and was one of his most precious memories. At first he was curious to find photographs of his mother when she was younger because all the ones he'd ever seen were torn down the middle, even the wedding photos. Then he realised it was his Nana who had ripped off his black and white supporting father from all photos. This photographic ethnic cleansing and all the other information interested him so much that he set about creating a family tree. But *Ancestry.com* or whoever were puzzled at first when the only information he wanted was his mother's side of the family. Like the parental photographs, his lopsided family tree would only have red and white branches.

It turned out that one day Marc's young amorous future father leapt over the wire fence in their garden into the loving arms of his new girlfriend, his mother. His Nana, as in her ethnically cleansing photographic future, had seen a pre–emptive opportunity for the genetic cleansing altogether of her son-in-law's family and football supporting line before he could marry her precious offspring and breed. She was to be bitterly disappointed when he landed safely in her daughter's arms. Almost in tears, she stammered to her husband: 'It's a pity the fence didn't catch the black and white bastard's bollocks.'

Marc loved his Nana.

And he never lost the angst over his rival team. Now he was sitting in the pub before yet another a Newcastle derby match in a medical and psychological mess.

Like every other home match day he had followed his routine and been driven the thirty-five miles to the match. He ate only cornflakes and a cup of tea for breakfast on a match day and then he'd eat his match day lucky meal - bacon, eggs and tinned tomatoes - at his Mam and Nana's house before hitting the pub. He never slept for three nights before a game and worrying about the next match started the minute the final whistle had blown at the previous one. He never spoke about the match he'd just seen in the pub or on the drive back home afterwards only of his worries about the next one. He never spoke to his wife at all about the match. He now needed many pills to keep him from worrying and prevent his stomach suffering the agonies of stress.

Ginger Gus, who lived to take the piss out of anyone and everyone, was telling a guy who had been coming to the pub and sitting next to them for weeks about his mate's psychological problems over supporting the team. This guy who had joined the asylum was a joy to Ginger Gus because he had a haircut like a German helmet with huge sideburns which he was so obviously proud of. He also wore a home-made jumper that Gus was sure his mother had knitted with a claw hammer. Ginger called him Ming the Merciless as he was the spit of the evil emperor. Ming wasn't over blessed with functioning neurones so he was puzzled when Gus had first introduced himself to the man with an enquiry about his hairdresser.

'Hi mate. I'm Gus. Been watching yeah and I love your haircut. Did your hairdresser use a lathe to cut it?'

Ming had looked puzzled. He had stroked his perfectly shaped *Jorman* helmet hair and replied to his new found *mate*, 'Nor mate. She used scissors. Divn't think she did woodwork at school like us lads. She did cookery.'

Gus had been overjoyed. *This gadgy was gonna be a gem* he chuckled to himself.

But now Ming was puzzled why Marc never seemed to enjoy himself so Ginger Gus attempted a psychological assessment of the tortured man.

'It's the match man. He's manic about it every day and every night until it kicks off and then he worries about the next one. At Wembley a few years ago I shared a room with the daft twat in St. Albans. Old Keith had driven down with seven of us in his car. He'd had to take the inside handles off to get us in. Marc must have had sixteen pints all day at least. Pissed in the car, pissed in the town - remember we'd been awake since four am to get the car and I canna remember when we got to beed. Marc's got six medicine bottles and strips of tablets lined up on the table. I woke up about four am desperate for a piss and mouth like a badger's arse. I torned ower and took a swallow of a half drunk can of lager and there was Marc, sat bolt upright in beed, staring at the wall. He looked at me and all he said was: *'You ginger twat. How the hell can you sleep? It's Wembley tomorrow.'*

Marc had heard the conversation and added his own part. 'The ginger bastard went back to sleep too. How could anyone do that on a match day?'

Ming the Merciless whispered to Gus: 'What's his wife think of it all?'

'She doesn't. It's like the Ripping Yarn tale *'Golden Gordon'*. Marc's son has to hide when he comes back from the match in case he throws a half brick at him and their lass always grabs the expensive clock in case he throws it through the window. The kids sit all day and night in their football strips trying to talk to him about the game or the lad's football news but he's gone to another world by them. He made the hospital take the sheets off his newborn son's cot because they had some black and white in them and he went home to get red and white ones. I think his wife may have been in emergency theatre at the time.'

Gus took a long slurp of his beer, leaving most of the froth on his bristly ginger moustache and continued his tales of his demented mate: 'His best one was that we were all drinking in Whitburn Cricket Club a couple of miles away from the ground. As kick off approached Marc was so worried about the match and wound up that we might not get there on time that he jumped in his car and took Keith and Billy to the match leaving John and me to jump a lift with a lad from the club. We piled into the ground sometime after and Marc is there nervous, twitching and manic, howling as usual at the team and referee as the match progresses. For some reason he suddenly realised – *Where's my son?* and he howled at me: *Where's our lad? Did you bring him with you?*

'I said: *'Nah, why would we have him? Didn't you tak him with you?'*

'He gans mental. *You left him in the club for God's sake, you daft ginger bastard!'* and he ran out of the ground only to find the stewards won't open the gates. By now of course he's lost the plot - as he does: *Open the ******** gate you fat bastards or I'll bury the pair of you. My seven year son is lost. Now open the ******** or else.*

'The stewards are faced with a red-faced, baldy, broken-nosed six foot four mental case and wisely opened the door. Marc ran to the car and drove all the way back to Whitburn Cricket Club where his seven year old son was sitting perfectly safe with a coke and a half eaten bag of crisps just where he'd left him thirty minutes before.'

Gus took another drink and commented: 'You couldn't make it up, man, totally forgot his own bairn because he's manic about the match.'

'Shut the hell up you ginger twat and get the beers in,' Marc affectionately butted in to Gus and Ming. 'The quiz is coming on soon.'

The pub held a quiz every Saturday which the friends always played to kill the time in between drinking. Gus took the hint that it was his turn and got up to go to the bar which was packed, worse than usual as it was Derby day.

John, Marc's great mate, had noticed that Dinky Derek's nine year old son was ripping up successive football cards that he pulled out of the *Match Attax* packets which his father had bought him. John asked him: 'What are you doing son?'

The reply was quick and acerbic: 'The black and white bastards! I'm not keeping any pictures of them.'

'Oh! Not keen on our opposition then son?' John rhetorically asked, thinking *Here we go, another borstal boy on the way* as he sat next to him with a beer.

'Don't squeeze in here you fat bastard,' the little angel said, growling at his *Match Attax* and tearing yet another Newcastle player card into several pieces.

'Don't talk to my boss like that,' spouted Derek, his dad, and he smacked his boy right around the head with a large tattooed hand. 'Sorry John. He's a lad isn't he?'

'Yup he's a lad alright Derek,' John replied, wondering how long it would be before he was following in his dad's footsteps. His dad was a good friend and colleague but pretty well daft on the team. And like Marc he had had a traumatic upbringing - his father and five brothers were all followers of Newcastle. They were all hard men and well known for causing trouble. As a result of his cultural isolation living among the enemy, Derek was rather emotionally and psychologically touched when it came to this competitive spirit between the two teams. He had no fear and often would be found in the opposition's manor and pubs singing and shouting his love for his team. Sadly, the numerous batterings received didn't seem to have much effect on father or son. And they were very much up for today's game.

The bar was filling up and the two tables of friends were about to settle into the quiz when the doors burst open and a man dressed in Army combat fatigues and full ski-mask balaclava ran in. He pulled out a steely black handgun, crouched down and shouted loudly over the cacophony:

'Get on the floor you bastards or I'll shoot.'

Those that heard and saw the deranged man fell under the bar tables and some threw themselves onto their families. Marc was about to throw a bottle at the crouching body in the hope it would distract him long enough to dive through the bar when the gunman stood up dropping his hand with the gun to his side. He pulled off his ski-mask and then, grinning from ear to ear through a huge black beard, he put his gun back in his flak jacket pocket and shouted to everyone in proximity taking cover from instant death: 'It's only me you daft buggers.'

And for sure it was only him – Crazy Jim.

Jim was known to many in the room but not to some of those who were still trembling and pretty angry. It didn't bother the mad bastard because things like that never did bother him. He was constantly up to some jape at the match and was a good mate of Marc and the boys. He put his mask in his pocket, released his pony tail and took off his coat, revealing the well-worked and strongly muscled body of the security man he was. His travelling mates Stan and Paul followed him to the two tables. They had driven a hundred miles or so from the North Midlands to get there. They usually travelled the length and breadth of the country to watch the team home or away.

'Had you going there didn't I?' laughed the big man as he sat down, pushing Derek's son even further along the seats.

The little cherub greeted the errant gunman with: '**** off you fat bastard. I'm not scared of your gun.'

'Charming manners they teach them these days,' Jim said, laughing.

'You bastard, I nearly spilt a pint because of you,' Old Keith piped up. 'What the hell have you got a gun for?'

'It's only a replica,' Jim answered and he took it out of the flak jacket pocket and handed it around.

'Bloody hell it's bloody realistic,' said Young Keith's brother who was serving in the army.

'Had some fun on the way up, didn't we lads?' Jim asked his two fellow passengers.

'Don't let me forget it,' said Stan, the driver of his BMW. 'We had our scarves hanging out the windows when a van full of Leeds on the way to their game came alongside. They wound the windows down and were challenging us to stop and fight. We gave them the finger but they kept accelerating and trying to cut us up. Jim says accelerate and get alongside them. So I do. Then the mad bastard pulls on his balaclava and takes out the gun from his pocket and winds the window down. He then sticks it in the face of the driver. The poor guy's face was a picture and the terrified passenger grabbed the wheel to swerve out the line of fire I guess. The van jerked to the left, off the carriage way and squealed to a halt on the banks of the A1.'

'Loved it: Pissed mesel,' Crazy Jim laughed, oblivious to the fate of his opposition fellow lunatics.

Amazed and shocked Young Keith asked: 'Crying out loud, how long have you had the gun mate?'

Young Keith was constantly amazed at the antics that the crew got up to at matches. He too had a difficult mixed race family life because like Marc and Derek he had married a lass from the dark side - Newcastle. At the wedding in Walker on Tyneside it had been pretty bleak. His new wife eight months pregnant and the Catholic priest who was not amused at their pre-nuptial sex reluctantly going through the motions; ten people from his side and ten from her side, all frozen solid. The priest, noticing them all shivering, apologised and informed them that the central heating pipes had been stolen. In Walker social club the reception was difficult, especially for Manic Marc, Keith's cousin, as 95 % of the drinkers were the opposition. The only good thing about the day Marc reckoned had been that Keith had managed to make passionate love to his new wife while she was vomiting into the toilet. He always was a romantic fool they say.

'He's not reet in the heed,' said Ginger Gus referencing Jim to a shocked Ming the Merciless, who was still recovering from the gun incident. Ginger continued: 'Last away match at Sheffield he wore dark glasses and carried a white stick. He spots a load of Wednesday supporters over the road and decides to have a laugh. He walks over and heads straight into them. As he approaches he's waving his white stick in front of him and swinging his free arm searching for unseen obstacles. He steams into the Sheffield lads hitting them on the shins and pushing them with his free arm. Wearing black sun glasses he moved his sightless head around like a white Stevie Wonder on Ecstasy and shouted: *'Who's that? Who's that? Can't you see I'm blind, man?'*

Gus continued to an astounded Ming: 'The lads all jump out of way off the narrow pavement some falling into the traffic; even they didn't want to hit a blind Sunderland supporter. Jim gets through them, lifts his glasses off onto his head turns to them all and shouts: *'Anybody seen me dog?'*

'And then as if a by a miracle he regains his sight and he runs straight into a bar that Stan and Paul had gone into across the road, dodging in and out of cars and buses with ease, much to the vexation of the Sheffield lads. There were lots of Sheffield lads standing as Jim came in and he's tapping his way with his white stick through to the bar. His mates had managed to get a seat and sat down waiting for their 'blind mate', and as usual, had brought with them a pack of cards ready to have a game. Crazy Jim orders three pints pushing a few people out the way and tapping their legs with his stick as he reaches the bar.

'The barman kindly told the boys to calm down and he poured the first pint and put it down on the bar: *There's your first one, mate. It's just to the left of you,* the caring landlord said to Jim who was staring up at the ceiling seemingly sightlessly. *Thanks mate,* Jim said and promptly turned to his right and supped up half of the pint stood on the bar belonging to another Sheffield punter. The shocked customer couldn't believe what had happened and stood looking very angry. The barman grabbed the lad's hand and pointed to the blind stick and apologised for his blind customer's mistake and suggested he'd pour him another pint.'

'Dear God he's mental man,' Ming uttered, looking over at a laughing Crazy Jim.

'Aye he is. Ah towld yeah. It gets better man,' said Gus and he continued. 'The barman poured two more pints for Jim and Jim carried his and then another pint to the table, knocking people out of the way each time with his stick and apologising profusely. He then went up to get the last pint and reached out for it but picked up the same lad's pint that the barman had refilled and promptly supped half of it again. Jim was staring ahead, oblivious of the man's purple face and looking through his dark glasses biting his tongue hard in case he laughed at the distraught man. The barman gesticulated at the man with his hands as if to say - *Calm down man, can't you see he's blind!*

'Jim picked up his last pint and walked through the crowded pub, stomping on people's feet, pushing the standing ones. Paul got up: *Heh man, outta the way, can't you see the man's blind. Give him some space,* and then he helped him to the table and they started playing cards.

'It doesn't take long for the big lad at the bar whose pint Jim had supped to see this and he shakes his head and says angrily to his mates: *Bugger this,* and he walks over, saying to Jim as he calmly lays down a prial of three sixes: *Ah thowt thou wor blind yeah Geordie bastard.*

'Jim still wearing his dark glasses stared at the ceiling and moved his head agitatedly around in a manner of, W*ho the hell is that?* Then he says, *I am blind. Who's that?'*

'The big lad says, *Eh up man, thou is playing t' cards man. Thou can't be t'blind.*

'Stan jumps up and sticks his face right in the aggrieved Yorkshireman's face. '*He is blind! We're using Braille cards. Are yeah daft or what?'*

Les took a swallow and smiled finishing his story. Ming was by this time staring at Gus in awe. As I said earlier, he wasn't over bright and didn't get the subtle Braille card humour so he questioned Gus: 'Where did they get the Braille cards, Gus? Ah've nivva seen them in a pub afor.'

Gus looked at his new found mate with the lathe shaped helmet hair and reverted to type, now bored of being civil to the challenged man. 'Yeah thick twat. It was a set up man. Ah thowt that haircut was ower heavy on your brains you daft twat.'

'Haway man, ah didn't get the joke did ah. Braille? Blind? Ha ha...funny. Bet the Sheffield gadgy didn't get that joke too did he?'

'Of course he did. Even thick Yorkshire folk could work that oot you daft bugger,' Gus grunted and, deciding his new victim wasn't worth the effort for a massive, relentless piss take - even he couldn't humiliate someone with a full frontal lobotomy - finished the tale quickly so he could move off to torture someone else. 'The Braille thing knocked the Sheffield lad back and he did consider maybe they were Braille cards for a few moments but he wasn't as thick as yeah and sussed they were taking the piss. So it didn't end well. But the crazy *blind* man taught his mates a useful clever ploy that hidden extendable coshes and fire extinguishers are handy weapons if yeah ivva need to get quickly out of a pub dispute caused by a near-sighted fracas.'

'Dear God,' Ming said, looking worried. 'What the hell will he be up to today?'

'God only knows but I won't be with him. I told you he's mental.'

Indeed, Crazy Jim was not with the unfortunate Gus when Gus was set alight by a fire bomb of sorts in the mayhem that erupted when ten thousand Magpie supporters were let out of the Roker End at the same time as the Sunderland fans. The Assistant Chief Constable of Northumbria's finest believed it was against their *human (?)* rights to keep them in. He seemed to realise the error of his ways because the next few derby matches were played without any away fans allowed in at all - the first time ever in British football.

And for both sets of fans spoiling the away Derby was tragic. It was definitely always a more special match for both tribes - but really always too intense. Other away matches were less frantic, less nerve racking and more fun.

Travelling to away grounds was the one day when thousands could break away from the tedium of school, work, looking after family or life on the dole and experience something new and exciting to normal surroundings. Many people have kept diaries or have amazing memories of away trips. Sadly for me, the drink and the devil have put paid to many of my memories. However, luckily many of my acquaintances from different clubs have retained the stories and experiences and I've taken great pleasure in weaving them into the fantasy of this narrative.

Some of the supporters of clubs I know travel thousands of miles and collect grounds like playing cards, some trying to get to that ultimate prize of attending all the grounds in the English league. As you may gather after Ginger Gus's description of Crazy Jim's antics, he had unique ways of achieving this milestone.

CHAPTER FOUR
Cardiff, Bristol City, West Brom & Big Ron Atkinson

Jim was a very poor teenager when he began a useful career in scamming football league grounds out of free tickets and hospitality. From these early beginnings he became the master of the football long con. It is little known but Albert Stroller and Micky Stone in *Hustle* were Crazy Jim's apprentices it is believed. Only those initiated into the Society for Psychopathic Con Men who have reached the level of the Royal Arch of Saint Nial really know the magical art.

When Jim was young and just an apprentice in the society he would write to the home club that Sunderland would be playing next and he'd tell them that their club would the 92nd and final league ground that he and his slightly strange mate. 'Mick Of A Thousand Stares', had visited. He then asked if they would allow the local newspaper to send a photographer to record the event. The photographer was a mate and also a phoney. Inevitably, the club would send an invitation and free hospitality. The three of them would arrive and be given a tour, tickets, team scarves and shirts, access to the executive bar and meetings with players and executives. At Arsenal they sat next to Doug Wetheral, a reporter working with the BBC and a Sunderland fan at heart. He absolutely cried with laughter at the pranks the two tricksters had played on so many of the league's top clubs. He proposed to tell the tale in his report on the game; a fitting monument to the ingenuity of the two young lads - if not their honesty.

WEST BROM

Crazy Jim believes his best day out at the 92nd league club scam was at West Brom. He wrote to them to say Mick and him were fans of football and had visited 91 grounds to watch the home teams and because West Brom was the last could they come and visit, take photos and publish them in their local newspaper. As usual the club fell for it and the con was complete when their charismatic manager of the time, Big Ron Atkinson, met them and gave them on a tour of The Hawthorns. He took them into the home dressing room and they met known Match of Day stalwarts of the time Cyrille Regis, John Wile, etcetera They then pestered the big man to let them meet the away team. So he changed the plan and took them into Sunderland's dressing room. As they walked in Gordon Chisholm said: 'Hello Jim, what the hell are you doing here?'

Jim quickly shut him up and Atkinson seemed not to have noticed. He said: 'It's not long to kick off boys. We still have to get your photo with me for our next programme. We'll do a special on you both.'

The famous manager led them to the centre circle with the club photographer and yet again they had Glen their mate, the fake newspaper photographer from their home town clicking away alongside the real photographer but as the two men waved to the crowds some of the away fans recognised them and began to chant their names. Big Ron looked at the crowd, waving and laughing and the reality that he'd been conned set in. He looked down at the three men. He was a big and threatening man and he growled: 'I thought there was a rabbit away when you wanted to meet all the Sunderland team.' He glowered, raised his clenched fist at them and after a second or two burst into smiles and waved towards the away crowd. 'Go on then you buggers. **** off to your Geordie mates.'

The happy con men did exactly that, running towards the laughing hordes encouraging them on. The stewards looked confused then panicked as they saw three lunatics running from the centre circle towards a packed away end. They obviously thought that they were West Brom lads on a suicide mission and they chased across after them. The Sunderland fugitives jumped into the waiting crowd just as the first stewards arrived but the way in was blocked to their pursuers by the first row of maniacs and the escapees enjoyed a warm welcome and a free match.

They wrote anonymously to West Brom for the next home programme within which sadly, and not unsurprisingly, the article on the 92nd club visit was missing. Amazingly, someone sent me this picture of their own scam. How they missed Crazy Jim, well, one will never know. There are some characters out there.

CARDIFF

Crazy Jim and 'Thousand Stares Mick' were desperate to get to a Cardiff v Sunderland promotion battle but it was sold out. Crazy Jim hatched yet another long con. The first part involved him persuading the local Hospital that his parents were elderly and that sadly both had fallen and needed wheelchairs. He then borrowed two chairs placing a deposit of a few pounds on them and purloined his mother's tartan picnic blankets to cover their legs.

The next step was travelling to Cardiff with the wheelchairs in the back of the van. When they arrived they sat in the wheelchairs, put the blankets over their legs and wheeled themselves to the ground. At the turnstiles the stewards asked for their tickets. As they didn't have any, they said they had come down on the bus with Sunderland Social Services and got separated from the care workers who had the tickets. The stewards let them in for nothing and wheeled them to the running track where they left them with the other real disabled Sunderland supporters, in front of the away end. A great result for the arch con men. But it all went wrong once Sunderland scored. Both of the intruders were up off the chairs jumping and celebrating with the red and white thousands behind them. The stewards came running over so the two likely lads abandoned the wheel chairs and leapt into the crowd. The cheering and laughing Sunderland supporters had seen the con men leap up from the wheelchairs and the stewards chasing them, so the crowd immediately sealed off the entry of the stewards.

After the game both men celebrated another successful scam to get into a packed ground. However, Jim had lost both the wheelchairs and so forfeited his deposits. However, the worst thing to happen to him was that his mam boxed his ears for losing her favourite tartan blankets.

BRISTOL CITY

The West Country is a long trip and the last thing you'd want to suffer is such a journey imprisoned in the boot of a Hillman Avenger. But it seems 'Mick Of A Thousand Stares', despite being a large, stocky, and slightly strange human being, was relatively happy to lie in the boot, smoking and snoring for six hours, jammed into a small space without any communication or food or water. This was because he had lost out in the lottery when six mates had drawn straws to see who would have to travel in the boot of the crammed car. He was a physical and mental wreck when he fell out at Bristol. They boys laughed, as you do, took the piss and they all piled off to the match.

Matches at Bristol were always lively. It must be the isolation from any normal culture and civilised human behaviour. This isolation and rejection means most people from the West Country are strange. Putting them into a football mob where they can actually mix with similar human beings was always risky. The vast quantities of mind-bending scrumpy they drink didn't help the situation much. Did you know that in the West Country real cider drinkers drink cider from porcelain tankards because the cider dissolves lead from pewter tankards? You didn't know that? Well, neither did the Bristol City fans, because they still used pewter tankards when Crazy Jim and 'Mick Of A Thousand Stares' arrived. A pewter tankard is a handy weapon if your muscular coordination and hippocampus have not been destroyed by lead poisoning. Not as useful as an extendable cosh, but heh, that's a moot point for those who study these things. My point is that in those days both Bristol teams' supporters were somewhat full of angst to see a new Homo species arrive in their evolutionary niche. The hallucinogenic intoxicating scrumpy, lead poisoning and pre-Stone Age tribal bonding always meant a lively reception to visiting fans.

Today had been no exception and on returning to the car the weary lads weren't looking forward to drawing straws again to see who would be jammed in the boot again for six or seven hours. And 'Mick Of A Thousand Unlucky Lotteries' lost again. He didn't even complain as he lit up a cigarette and climbed in his tomb – resting his head on the petrol tank. And he didn't even complain when the petrol tank blew up!

Crazy Jim moved on from scamming UK clubs to the bigger challenge of those in Europe. As a Sunderland supporter this was an infrequent occurrence over the past sixty years, but International football with National teams offered him a huge challenge. So much so that he began applying his hard-won skills to World Cup and Euro games...

CHAPTER FIVE
Germany, Mackems In Milan, & Kidnapping in Peterlee

As I write, warm, sunny and beautiful locations for most UK football supporters are just a negative Covid test and two weeks quarantine dream away. For 95% of all Football League teams, Europe is just a President Macron veto away. And as I scribble, I have yet to see a Mackem in Milan and maybe that is not a bad thing for the post-Brexit settling in of the warring tribes.

A lady friend of John told him that she had travelled to Amsterdam for a pre-season match. The train was packed with supporters and a friendly Dutchman asked a Sunderland fan where he was from. The Sunderland supporter said: 'Suth'ick'.

Needless to say the Dutchman looked puzzled. Never mind - the Dutchman could not be expected to know the districts of a provincial town in the United Kingdom. He also would have no idea that Mackem language is quite different to Durham pitmatic or Tyneside Geordie. Suth'ick', or sometimes for the even more parochial 'Sudd'ick', means Southwick.

The Dutchman said: 'I'm sorry I don't know that place.'

The supporter stared at the man astonished and stammered out: 'How man, you divn't knar where it is? It's near Marley Potts man!'

Yes. Maybe Europe isn't ready yet for some team's supporters.

When John heard this story he asked the lass did this guy have ginger hair and a tash. And curiously he did. *Another theory proven* he thought.

International matches were always exciting and especially World Cup days out in Europe. Crazy Jim became expert at getting tickets for these matches and many others. He was a master at avoiding trouble with either the police or opposing fans but some of his inventions to avoid bother and get into grounds without tickets sailed a bit close to the legal winds of most countries. For the 2006 World Cup in Germany he and two sons carried alternative sets of licence plates in the car they drove over to the

Fatherland. They carried a fake GB one for borrowing free fuel from petrol stations on the way and French ones for parking up in Germany. Crazy Jim thought they would stop the car being attacked by the German thugs who were voicing off in the media that the Dutch and English were their targets.

The first port of call was Nuremberg and they pulled up in a convenient backstreet and changed the plates to the French ones. They had England tee-shirts and had written on each one, 'English ticket wanted'. They approached a row of bars full of England fans and everyone cheered, but no tickets. It took three days of solid drinking with the fans for the first part of their plan to unravel. Surprisingly, the success of the latest scam took an American, and amazingly, a Sheffield Wednesday player at that. He had been signed by *The Owls* but had never made the grade and had left for his homeland. He'd returned to Germany for the tournament with an astonishingly full-breasted partner and when he saw the tee-shirts and the three lads all looking a bit miserable he sat down to chat. His partner, of course, took most of the lad's attention away from the boring Yank's conversation but when the words 'Spare ticket' were mentioned Crazy Jim perked up and asked if he would like to sell it. The guy gave it away as he had been sent a few from Sheffield and didn't need this one. *Great luck* Jim thought now he could begin to implement the great World Cup ticket scam.

Jim had concocted this *long con* hustle some weeks before in England but it required a genuine ticket to launch it. Now he had the ticket. The tournament was supposed to be the most policed World Cup event in history due to the number of hooligan groups travelling from all over Europe and the media spoke of 'Rings of steel around grounds' with huge police presences and ticket control at its highest level. Therefore to get into grounds with no ticket, which was Crazy Jim's speciality, would require great attention and skill. The first part of the wily grifter's plan had been to *acquire* a medical shoulder sling and crutch and two German Red Cross letter headings onto which he had printed in German descriptions of the various medical treatments for his two friends' osteopathic problems.

The plan required Jim to use the free ticket generously donated by the Yank to enter the ground and then meet up with his mates from Shotton Colliery who would donate their used tickets as the next phase of the master plan. He'd reconnoitred the stadium over a couple of days and knew there was a perimeter wire fence with gaps where he could pass the used ticket through to his first son.

On entry to the ground with the real ticket he met the crazy men from Shotton and one gave him his used ticket. Jim went to the prearranged place to pass the ticket to his first son and made his way to the turnstile Jim had entered by - one of those that the England fans were allocated. His son after receiving the ticket had put on the shoulder sling had taken up the crutch and then limped in false pain to that turnstile.

Meanwhile back in the ground, Jim had grabbed a steward near the turnstile and had acted in a panic trying to explain his angst and horror: 'It's my son. He fell down in the ground and the Red Cross have taken him for treatment. I've lost him and his mother will kill me if I don't get him back.'

Then as his crippled son approached the turnstile he shouted in joy and pointed to the prodigal offspring. 'Look it's a miracle he's been cured and he's here!'

The steward looks over at the lad standing with sling and crutch clearly in pain and Jim says: 'Quick. Can you help get him back to me please?'

Another steward has by now heard this and come over to enquire and help his mate. His mate tells him the story and the other steward who was a bit more Teutonic and cynical asked to see Jim's ticket, which Jim happily showed him and then asked Jim's son through the bars if he was ok.

'Yes, I'm fine now the Red Cross have helped me. I really want to watch the match and see my Dad,' replied the resurrected Lazarus.

'Ok, let me zee your ticket,' the more suspicious steward asks and Jim's son hands him the ticket which the steward promptly puts through the machine. It comes up as *used*. Thinking he's caught the evil English out the steward exclaims to Jim: 'Ah, ziss ticket is used. Nein entry!'

Crazy Jim, cleverer than his Hun antagonist, calmly explained the problem. 'Of course it is mein friend. He used it to get into the stadium didn't he. He was in the ground when he fell.'

The German, was well, German, so he was not convinced by mere words. He needed documents and he turned to Jim's son through the bars and asked, 'Ver are zee medical papers?'

Jim's son produced the forged Red Cross papers they'd prepared back home. The SS guard - I'm sorry slip of the politically correct stereotype tongue there - the steward, looked at the paperwork suggesting post-treatment advice and, clueless as to the meaning of the German medical terminology but happy with the official Red Cross stamp, handed the sheet back and opened the gate saying: 'Ziss is all in order. Alles gut hier. Please come through.'

The nice steward smiled at Crazy Jim and his pain-racked son and put his thumb up and said: 'Alles ist gut?'

'Wye aye. Alles ist gut marra. Danke schön,' Jim replied trying hard to keep his laugh in.

They moved on with Jim holding his son upright as he limped around the corner - straight into the bar. Laughing uncontrollably they supped a stein of lager each and then went to the other turnstile to repeat the process with the brother.

Unable to contain their joy when all were reunited they strolled to another bar and as it was a sunny blue sky and they felt marvellous and were looking forward to the match, they decided to have a photo taken. A lady passed them by and Jim called her back and asked if she'd take a picture. She was English which helped and the three of them linked arms and one of the boys held up the scam ticket in front them for the posterity of the photograph. She obliged but was curious to know why they were laughing so much. Innocently, they began to tell her the story of the long con. She listened to most of it before screwing up her face and putting her fingers in her ears. She was laughing she said: 'No! No, don't tell me anymore. I'm police! You crazy buggers stop and bugger off before I get done for collaboration.'

It seems she was a police hooligan spotter from Birmingham City and Aston Villa. How she never *spotted* Crazy Jim is anybody's guess!

England won and Crazy Jim and his sons carried on the same long con at all the other matches until England were knocked out by Portugal in the quarter finals. This result was an inevitable conclusion for a book on the relentless misery of football fans because England fans have suffered as long as most misery fans, fifty five years in fact and football has yet to come home. We'd hoped this summer once the Covid bug went away provided a brave new Scotland didn't spoil the homecoming. It didn't completely and they didn't but the trophy didn'a come home at last either. Instead in the final the Italians took it back to Rome courtesy of three missed England penalties.

I know Crazy Jim was plotting long con ticket scams for the Euros but hopefully this time his wife packed the correct items in his bag. For the last Euro trip she made a slip up that needed all the humble man's slick advocacy and ingenuity to avoid the long arm of the law. This is the tale of a man's simple personal travelling items nearly causing a terrible miscarriage of justice.

It all started when Crazy Jim explained to his wife he was travelling to England from his work in France to meet his two sons who had hired a camper van to travel over to Europe for the matches. His beautiful and caring wife had packed his bag for him and placed in it all the things she thought he'd need for his adventure and football fest. At the airport he was about to go through security when he was taken aside by two Gendarmes and placed in an interview room. *Oh dear* he thought *they must know me!*

One of the guards got excited and started banging the table. He could see his travel bag on the table and the guard looked menacingly at it. The guard asked if Jim had anything he shouldn't in it. Jim knew it contained nothing but a few toilet things and personal hygiene products so he grinned and told the man there was nothing to worry about. His grinning seemed to take the guard over the edge and into some Gallic frenzy so he hurled abuse in French and reached inside the bag.

To the smiling detainee's horror the guard pulled out Jim's favourite extendable cosh with the hard rubber ball on the end.

'These ees yours?' he shouted in broken English.

Jim looked him in the eyes and thought *Well it is actually mine but it shouldn't be there - what the hell I may as well tell him the truth.*

'It is mine, yes, but I've no idea how it got in my bag,' Jim explained.

The guard rants on and on and in Jim's basic schoolboy French he realises he is about to be locked up on the spot. He looked at the disturbed guard who appeared certain to die of apoplexy with red face and bulging neck blood vessels. Eventually the Gallic mad man cools down and Jim asks him could he make a phone call before they take him off to Devil's Island and a long spell with his cell mate Papillion. Surprisingly, they let him make the call to his darling wife.

'Hello dear, I'm about to be locked up. Did you put my favourite extendable cosh in my bag?' he gently asked down the phone, as one would if the local law enforcement had found an extendable cosh in one's toilet bag.

'Of course I did. Remember we watched that program on TV about all the trouble that was planned for Russian, French and Italian fans to attack England fans and I asked do you need your cosh packing and you said you did.'

Jim thought for a moment *I'm not stupid enough to ask her to pack the....'*

And then he realised what had happened. He had answered his caring wife's question with heavy sarcasm and said to her: 'Yes of course I'll take it. Put it in my hand luggage, I'm bound to get that through security for a flight to England.'

Sarcasm was lost on his precious, so she lovingly packed it for her dearest's protection from harm from the nasty foreigners. You may well ask what else would a loving wife do but pack your extendable cosh with the hard rubber ball in with the toothpaste and roll on deodorant. You have to shed a little tear at the devotion to her husband's safety. Everyone should have a partner who looks after your personal health and wellbeing with such love as Crazy Jim's wife.

The outcome was that Jim told his guards of what had happened. He had opened up the confession with, 'You are going to laugh at this...' and surprisingly after a bit of translation between them and dour looks at Jim they both burst out laughing. The less deranged one said: 'No one could make that up. You can go.'

Jim realised that he only had ten minutes to get through to his flight and his sons were waiting for him. They took sympathy and hijacked a VIP cart and took him past security and passport control straight onto the tarmac and the airplane. Sitting on the back of the cart, unseen by the guard driving, Jim could not stop laughing at this surreal turn around and his lucky emancipation.

He said goodbye and thanks to the guard and climbed the airplane steps to freedom. He turned around and shouted down to the official.

'How do I claim my cosh back when I fly home?'

The Frenchman took out his silver handcuffs and waved them at the crazy Anglais and mouthed the one phrase he knew perfectly well in English. '**** off.'

Jim sat on the plane and took his glass of champagne and chuckled at his escape and the bizarre events. But his happiness turned to sadness when he realised he'd never see his beloved possession again. It had seen him through twenty years of travels and escapades with England and Sunderland. He shed a small tear. Well, doesn't everyone cry a little when you lose your favourite extendable cosh? It's only natural.

Ginger Gus was always convinced Crazy Jim was not quite right in his head and as I must continue with more of these stories I worry about most of the players in this book and my own sanity. But they have to be told, so we'll carry on until the Duly Authorised Officer finally knocks on the door and slaps that section 135(2) on me – so here's another one for the casebook.

BRIGHTON

Europe is either a dream away or a National team adventure for most of us. Normality is travelling to familiar grounds in the rain, sleet and darkness and extracting every bit of fun out of a day and night out watching our favourite teams. For the Northern lads travelling away in the UK, the South Coast or even the South West is most the exotic destination they'll ever see. And some of the more obscure country towns that they can invade either before or after the match are much more welcome than trips to Oldham, Coventry, Hull and the like.

On a long trip to the seaside town of Brighton in the sunny Deep South the lads had taken the famous overnight Frankie's bus. They picked up a lad from Wakefield at 2.00 am and he sat next to a bloke who, although clearly pissed, was in a very morose mood. The 'Wakey' man asked him what was wrong and the sad man answered: 'Ah divn't even like football man.'

'Then why are yeah ganning then?'

'The bastards have kidnapped me. I was walking from the pub after closing time to the chip shop for me and our lass's supper. It was pissing down and this bus pulled up and asked if ah'd like a lift. Champion, I thowt, but next thing I knaar I'm heading down the A19 to ******* Brighton.'

The lad must have enjoyed himself because the next time our Wakefield man met him he was seen clutching and cuddling a woolly toy horse and rolling around drunk in the little town they had invaded on the way back from Brighton. He garbled out in his drunkenness that he'd acquired the toy horse somewhere he couldn't remember in an attempt to appease their lass when he finally got back sometime Sunday morning. He was whining in his misery: 'Two days missing and I only went to get some fish and chips man. She'll murder me.'

And I guess that sums up some away trips. Those who don't go can never see the reason to leave long before the match kicks off and come home many days after either voluntary or as a prisoner of fate. The match is co-incidental to the enjoyment. Far too many times I couldn't even remember the match at all. But maybe that was a blessing.

In the old days drink and the entertainment before match days was wide and varied. Some towns put on cultural extravaganzas for their own and opposition fans. Newcastle was no exception and as befitting a multi-cultural oasis that *the Toon* always was, the German Hoffbraus Bierkeller was open before a home match to all travellers who wished to experience the warm Geordie/Jorman culture first hand. So we'll move on to the Teutonic and exotic dancer wonderland that was Newcastle before the Nottingham Forest cup tie some time ago.

CHAPTER SIX
The Hofbrauhaus, Nottingham Forest & Aston Villa

'Ah just kna'd that was gonna happen,' Mick sighed. 'This'll cause it to kick off. They'll arl gan mental and I just knar ah'll end up knackered.'

The usual gloomy cloud that hung over him had just opened up and drenched him with even more misery as he poured out his worries to the two mates standing with him in the Leazes End at St James Park.

And sure it enough it did *kick off* as half the Leazes End invaded the pitch and charged across towards the visiting Nottingham Forest supporters, having a few slight altercations with the Forest players as they went.

'Aye,' Davey replied. 'It always happens when the lads have had ower many. Come on let's get out and into the pub afor we arl get locked in. The poliss will abandon this.'

John followed them past the scattered remnants of the packed Leazes End and thought, *Well there's another fun day out with my Newcastle mates. I knew it was gonna be one of them days when we went to the Bierkeller before the match. Why do I keep doing this?*

He did it because he sometimes went with his friends from home, school and also his football playing team mates to watch Newcastle United. Always it seemed to end up with *fun and frolics.* Today he had gone to watch the Newcastle v Forest in the 6th round FA cup after playing football himself in the morning. They ended up in the Hofbräuhaus where lots of supporters always ended in getting absolutely tanked up before the match. Match days were particularly special as the *Jorman bierkeller'*employed lady strippers to while away the pre-match nerves.

'The lads are enjoying themselves today,' Davey said. 'Looks like ower fifty thousand sell oot and most will be pissed the way this is ganning. Look at the clip of that bugger?'

The three of them looked over at a young lad with his shirt ripped off by a stripper, trying to cuddle and kiss her. He was covered in tattoos and black and white paint with his shaved head painted with '**** *the Mackems*'.

'Aye, met him on the bus tee Birmingham a few weeks ago. He nivva got back on after the match. Must have been locked up,' Mick said.

'Nee surprise there, looking at the clip of him,' Davey agreed.

The whole place was heaving and rocking. Songs bawling out and shouts of, 'United, United!' and the lady performers were valiantly trying to entertain the masses. A peculiar form of entertainment for Saturday lunchtime you may think.

The crazy man became too amorous and the stripper kneed him in his gonads. Two bouncers came on and dragged him off. The customers began getting rowdy and hurling abuse and objects at them.

'This is gonna get naughty soon,' John said, having seen it all before.

'Aye, let's hope the next stripper is more ladylike eh?' Davey replied, smiling and taking another big swig from his Stein of lager.

After an interval the masses had been calmed by a few bouncers and the waitresses' affections, and the new stripper did indeed come on. She was dressed in bondage gear and carried a large whip.

The crowd howled.

Mick said in his most laconic way: 'Ah just kna this'll gan tits up.'

Mick lived in perpetual misery believing like *Chicken Licken* that the sky was about to fall upon him anytime. Forty-six years later as I write the story when he sat with his bucket list mate he still feels the same but this time he was correct - the sky did fall in.

The stripper asked for someone to come up and help her with her act.

'Oh dear, he disn't look arl there in the heed,' John said, as a long, tall, skinny lad with mucky brown, straggly long hair and baggy jeans hanging off his backside and a long stuck-out jaw like Desperate Dan, climbed onto the stage to chants from two tables of his mates: 'Gan on Jimmy! Show hor yeah cock.'

He took off his denim shirt and posed for the audience, his thin wiry body and small beer belly causing one of them to shout. 'She's dying for yeah body man.' This prompted the whole lot of them to start singing: 'Get your cock out for the lads.'

'If that gormless looking imbecile starts waving his todger around I'm outta here,' Davey said, twisting his face into a vision of pain.

Luckily, before he could extract his organ the stripper came over and grabbed the throw back, rubbing her body up against him. She picked his shirt from his hands and threw it onto the two tables of his howling mates. She pushed him away gesturing to the grinning imbecile with her whip that she would soon be administering some pain to him. He stood staring at her vacant like while the mob urged her on. She cracked the long whip across the stage, came close to him and licked him up and down his body. He started to grab her but she pushed him away. The mob chanted and banged their tables.

'Ah just kna, I've got a feeling this isn't gonna end ower good John,' Mick muttered.

'Aye, look at his fyess man. Hasn't got a clue what to dee or what's happening. He's not a full shilling. Ah towld yeah, he's not reet in the heed that bugger,' John said.

The dominatrix strutted around winding the mob up and dragging her whip along the stage, wiggling leather cupped breasts at the boy. He tried in vain to grab one and missed with his mates chanting and encouraging him by shouting loving words of romantic comfort: 'She's teasing you man. Get stuck in to her, you soft twat.'

The stripper got behind the imbecile and looking at the audience and pulled the whip back, extending her arm ready to launch a soft lash. She smiled at the audience, put her head to one side and opened her hands in a gesture meaning, *Should I do it boys?*

His mates all shouted: 'Gan on! Howk the soft bastard.'

The lady swings the whip, gently strokes the lad over the back with a small crack stands back and smiles at everyone, parading her breasts and body around. The chastised lad jumped in the air clutching behind him and shouting: 'Ow! That hurt. Why'd yeah dee that yeah cow, I'll knack yeah.' And he runs over to the poor matron of pain, picks up the whip, knocks her down on the floor and starts thrashing her with it, like some deranged Captain Bligh of *Munity on the Bounty.*

'Ah just knew it,' Mick wailed. 'Let's get out of here afor we get dragged into this shite.'

And sure enough he was correct. The bouncers flew onto the stage and laid into the aggrieved patron. Obviously the subtleties of sadomasochism were lost on his simple mind. Cue his mates piling onto the stage and getting stuck into the bouncers while the stripper's car driver quietly slipped on stage and dragged her by her feet off the stage.

The three boys drank off quickly and left the mass brawl and sprawling bodies. As they left the mayhem they could hear the melodic and haunting melody emanating from the chanting of the non-combatants to the outnumbered bouncers: *'You're going home in a ********* ambulance.'* They made a quick exit up into the town and when safely well away from the nutters, they fell into *The Blackie Boy* in the Bigg Market.

'It nivva changes does it. Iviry time you bring me here it gans mental,' John said to his two mates, squeezed against the wall of the packed pub.

'Ah just knaar, it might kick off at the match. It's just my luck man,' Mick mumbled discontentedly.

And again he was correct. It started with the usual antics of the packed Leazes End stand. The wave of fresh urine flooding down the terraces into their shoes was a bonus. John stood amazed watching as it ebbed and flowed down the steps. There were 54,000 fans in the ground and John was sure there must only be one netty.

And then the police fell for the same trick they always fell for. John suspected they had never been trained watching *Columbo* or *Kojak* because they fell for it every time. Someone in the middle of the crowd behind the goal, where the biggest concentration of lunatics outside of Bedlam stood, called for a policeman to come over to help with some trouble. He duly does. Cue getting his helmet pinched and attempts to get his truncheon. It kicks off and the policeman is rapidly surrounded. Further policemen then start pouring into the crowd. Cue a mass battle with the poliss surrounded by the lads cuddling and comforting them with their Dr Martens, enjoying their little jesting. Sometime later it calms, bodies are ejected from the crowd and the ground and everyone gets back to watching the match.

Nottingham Forest score again; it's 1-3 and Pat Howard is sent off. The crowd begins to rumble like a volcano and that's where this story began with Mick's prediction of doom: 'Ah just kna'd that was gonna happen.'

And sure enough the crowd got more and more boiling.

Then a huge fat guy climbed out of the right side of the front of the Leazes End and onto the pitch, stripped off his shirt, huge chest and belly covered in Newcastle tattoos, and steamed into the police trying to stop him. A massive punch-up set off with him getting the better of the police until more jumped on him and then about 600 to 700 of his fellow loonies erupted from the volcano and jumped onto the pitch to give him a hand. Then, possibly as an afterthought, they ran across the pitch to have a friendly chat with their Forest chums in the Gallowgate End - lamping a few players on the way.

The referee, Gorden Kew, stopped the game and when it restarted Newcastle equalised and came back to win 4-3. Forest and the FA both believed that the linesman was too scared to rule the winning goal offside; hence, they had to replay the match. Which surprisingly for Mick, they won.

On the way home the lads stopped off in a pub when they opened and heard on the radio that thirty-nine fans were charged, twenty-three hospitalised (two with fractured skulls) and a hundred and three treated for minor injuries – and one young lady dressed in a rubber suit, mask and leather boots, still holding onto a whip, was treated for shock.

NOTTINGHAM FOREST

A couple weeks later Manic Marc had travelled to Nottingham Forest on the Washington Gardener's Social Club bus. The match ended 2-2 and afterwards there was mayhem. Those days, anyone who came from the North East was called a Geordie. Only diehard Newcastle fans brought up in the shipyards on the Tyne would call Sunderland fans Mackems and differentiate themselves as Geordies. Many older people attended both football clubs, alternating each week; most with a loyalty to one team but happy to watch another. It was changing violently around the late sixties and early seventies, the time Marc was in Nottingham, but to many being Geordie meant coming from Northumberland or Durham. The point of this story is that Nottingham Forest supporters were not so clued up on North East regional geography or tribal sectarianism. Geordies were Geordies, and Sunderland people were no different to those that had put so many of them in hospital only a couple of weeks ago. It was payback time.

The Trent Bridge was often the scene of ambushes on away fans by many gangs of Forest supporters and Marc realised that it would be the better part of valour to slip away with his mate Billy, leaving Sunderland supporters thronging over the bridge, and slip away walking along the embankment underneath. He was approaching a policemen standing under the bridge when he saw a body tumbling down off the bridge. It landed in the River Trent with a loud splash. The drowning man was clearly in distress and Marc saw that he had a Sunderland scarf on. The policeman had been standing next to a lifebelt and rope and he threw it in to the struggling man who grabbed it and the policemen pulled him to the bank. Marc and Billy helped the distressed bloke out. He had been beaten and thrown over the bridge by Forest lunatics.

Marc turned to policeman and thanked him and said: 'Lucky you were standing there mate.'

'I always stand here. They do that to away supporters every match.'

Marc looked at the man in amazement. 'Why the **** don't you stand on the bridge then and stop the bastards.'

'I'm not doing that. It's dangerous up there.'

A very sensible, or a very cynical man, you may say.

Standing in the wrong position can often get policemen caught out. It may be hard to believe for some but the following year Sunderland played both Manchester United and Aston Villa in the Second Division (Championship for the millennium bairns among you) and also York and Carlisle. An eclectic mix for sure.

Aston Villa and Sunderland had been playing each other since the dawn of the Football League and between them they shared the league title on numerous alternate seasons in those halcyon heady days we remember so well - before the Boer War. At the time, like Newcastle, they were still considered *giants* in the game. Well, they were actually becoming a bit softer and smaller giants. Now they are more like The Big Friendly Giant (BFG) in the Sky TV Giant Country and live amongst the evil foreign giants, Chelsea Fleshlumpeater and his mates, the Man City Bonechruncher, the Man Utd Child Chewer and the Arsenal Maidmasher - horrible buggers who completely changed the BFG's nutrition from grizzle-filled cold meat pies and lukewarm Bovril to Snozzcumbers and Prawn Sandwiches. A nightmare indeed for all young children and unlike the storybook, good Queen Bessie won't rescue us from the evil Giant Country in The Sky, so I'll have to move back to real football time and the story long before Snozzcumbers took over from hairy meat pies.

There were 57,000 people in Villa Park that day. Sunderland had to win to get promoted. Davey and Mick had repaid John the doubtful compliment of taking him to watch the Newcastle v Forest FA Cup World War and driven him down the M6 from Manchester to watch this massively important match. The problem was the ground was full. It is estimated well over another three thousand locked out Sunderland fans were trying to get in. So the three likely lads and many more were milling around trying to find a weakness in Villa Park's defences.

'Lads, are you looking to get in?' a woolly-hatted, older man collared them and asked.

'Aye,' said John.

'Well, some of the lads have been bunking over the wall just past that turnstile. There's a gap in the spikes on the top - worth a try.'

So they jogged around to where they saw a group of about six lads and one lass giving each other hand ups and stands on their shoulders. One by one they reached the top, cocked their legs over the wall and disappeared over the wall into the black hole below.

'Let's give it bash,' John said.

'Ah just kna, I'll break me neck,' Mick whined. 'Killing mesel to watch bloody Sunderland; just knew this trip was wrang.'

John comforted him: 'Oh shut yer gob man, you'll love it. It's character building.'

'Howay then,' Davey said, 'let's get ganning. It's five to three. I'm not driving arl the way doon here to watch ******** Sunderland and then sit out here with nee pub open. You'se giz a bunk up.'

Mick cupped his hands and lifted him onto John's shoulder and Davey grabbed the top of the wall and peered over into the hidden masses on the other side. John shouted: 'What's the drop like? Nee poliss?'

'Nor; it's clear but it's a lang drop. **** it I'm ower,' and he cocked his leg over the wall and slid over.

'It's your turn Mick. I'll give yeah a bunk,' Davey said to his troubled mate.

'Ah just kna I'll die. For ****'s sake why do I do this with yeah two lunatics? I canna reach the top man.'

'Dee yeah's want a hand?' A large grizzly looking man standing with another big man and his two children had noticed the problem that without three people they could never reach the top.

'Aye, cheers marra,' John said, thinking he should have thought of that. The ten cans on the way down were talking their effect. The human chain got Mick to the top. He looked over, cried his last, 'Ah just kna...' and slipped over. John was next; he was handed onto the other man's shoulders, slipped his leg over the wall, placed two hands on the top and slid down the wall onto the other side – straight on top of a waiting policeman.

The policeman was, like Robert Plant in Led Zepplin, *Dazed and Confused* and squashed flat out. The other policeman who had been sent over to stop the invading hordes clambering over the battlements was also knocked over.

John luckily was unhurt and despite the many pints was onto his feet quicker, stepped over *the sleeping policeman*, not slowing down to 10 mph by the way (subtle traffic reference there folks) and hurtled away from the long outstretched arms of Birmingham's finest, and only conscious law, straight into the helping arms of Birmingham's finest mental case hooligans.

Sadly, John in his hurry to escape instant hospitality from Aston's Old Bill had ran towards the fenced Villa lunatics who were cheering the hapless invader on and shouting: 'Over here mate, jump in here, we'll save you.' And of course they did, but only after a few *friendly* pats on the back and assisting him in his violent attempts at running towards his own supporters with a *helpful* toe cap push. Into the red and white hordes he leapt, just as the police ran up. The crowd parted like The Red Sea allowing their own particular Moses to lose himself amongst them while they closed upon the chasing men in blue and squashed them yet again like Ramses and his chariots all those seasons ago.

Of course, Sunderland lost and with it went the chance of promotion. The three met up again at Davey's car and headed up the M6 along with the thousands of other travelling supporters. Many, many depressed but some quite a lot happier as they were heading to Blackpool for the night to rape and pillage, living the Viking heritage they shared - as you do.

CHAPTER SEVEN
Firebombs, West Ham and Wembley

Some memories, like poor Mick's of the Bierkeller fracas and some of the crazy people I knew, should really be buried deep in my sub consciousness but every now and then I have a geriatric, drug-induced dream of the good old days. Frightening images of past acquaintances drift through my unconscious sleep. Happily, I had a good dream last night of Les, a ginger-haired friend and neighbour of mine from my home village with whom I shared many fun days when we were young. This prompted me to contact him again after some years and see if he had survived this torturous world. And indeed, he has, and sent me pictures of his lovely granddaughter. All of which stimulated me get off my sick bed and write about another strawberry blond, Les's his alter ego, the character Ginger Gus. We left him a few pages ago just after he'd been fire bombed by his mortal enemy, 'The Mags'.

I continue: after the Derby match...

Ginger Gus was only mildly burnt when the fire bomb hit him after the Newcastle derby. He was lucky, unlike the West Ham supporter with whom the Magpies had perfected their firebomb technique when hurling one into the jolly Cockney supporters at St James Park a few years before. This event spurned a great piece of musical and literary excellence to rival those great Newcastle bands, Dire Straits and The Police – so, to the tune of The Ramblers song, *'I'm only a poor little sparrow'*:

The Leazes End ode to West Ham

> *He's only a poor little Hammer,*
> *He came for a fight,*
> *So we set him alight,*
> *And now he won't come anymore.*

Gus was rescued by a horde of South Shields Sunderland supporters outside the Roker Pie shop.

Ginger Gus often had some amazing luck - probably the Devil does look after his own, as he was often saved by the bell. He could cause the next world war with his japes and piss taking but rarely did he end up harmed from it, apart from his lass's retribution, which of course would be terrible for any normal man. And when he returned to the bar with his ginger locks slightly singed Manic Marc had little sympathy for him.

'We should have but yeah in a bogie got some pennies for the guy and left you teh burn. It would have paid for the round you missed. It's your torn. Get them in yeh tight ginger bastard.'

Yes, Gus could cause a fight with a tame mouse. And the weekend of the Sunderland v Norwich League Cup final he excelled in his more eccentric behaviours.

Tony was a part time neutral supporter of football who claimed that he had only been to one match, Newcastle v Man United and never thought of going to an away match but he was a work colleague of Old Keith who had the potential to be his new boss so Keith had invited him on the tour to Wembley to impress him. Sadly, he wasn't reckoning on Ginger Gus.

There were seven in Keith's Austin Allegro company car and they were heading down on the Saturday before the Sunday final, hoping to get to St Albans, where they planned to stay, not long after opening time. To fit them all in Keith had taken the window handles and arm rests off the insides of the car - yes, this was in the days before electric windows folks. He then picked up the lads one by one starting about 6 am.

Gus was still tight from the night before pre-Wembley celebrations drinking in Sunderland and had to make a quick dash from the house in case he woke up his wife.

They arrived at Tony's posh house at East Herrington. Tony was waiting outside his back garden gate. Gus said to Keith that he was bursting to go to toilet as he'd done a runner before his wife could chastise him for the night before. He squeezed out of the car and said to an astonished Tony: 'I'm borsting mate. Can I use yr back garden?'

Tony had never met Gus and looked shocked at this strange request to relive himself in a trim suburban garden, but in the spirit of *Well it is a lad's day out* he said: 'Yes, ok then, just go in but don't let my wife or bairns see you please and don't do it on her lawn please it's her pride and joy.'

'Champion marra. Ah winnit be lang,' said a desperate Gus and he opened the gate and went in. Tony waited anxiously watching in case his wife or neighbours saw his new found *marra* exposing himself and the journey was cut short by an early arrest. Gus came back and jumped into the back of the car looking happy. Tony came back staggering, stammering and stuttering to his work colleague plainly in a state: 'My neighbour and her kids were watching through the kitchen window man. It was bloody horrible. What kind of bloke diz that man. And on the wife's flowers for God's sake!'

'For ****'s sake man, get in the car you soft bugger. We've got a match to gan tee and we're late and me guts are arl ower the place worrying. We haven't time to bother with that. Surely the wifey has seen a grown man having a piss before?' Marc shouted at the distraught man, swallowing another antacid tablet.

'He didn't have a piss,' the poor man barely uttered, still in catatonic shock. He slumped against the car clearly in shock, dumping the nice neat bag of sandwiches his wife had made for him on the ground. He looked positively wiped out with it all.

'Haway man. Get in the car. Bah, ah needed that. Didn't have time when I got up and me arse was borsting with arl that curry from last neet,' Gus said, fastening his belt and slapping the devastated man on the back, oblivious to anything wrong with his outdoor number two ablutions. 'Any one got a can open yet?'

'He shit in our lass's flower bed man. Why would anyone do that?' Tony stammered out to anyone who might care.

Gus explained, looking slightly puzzled as to what this new posh guy's problem was: 'Yeah towld me not to dee it on your lass's lawn. Anyway, it's canny fertilizer man and free.'

'Tony, stop twisting man and let's get on the road. Its awnly thirty-six hours to the match man. And you're worrying about a bit of shite in your garden,' Marc shouted back at the distraught suburban man.

Tony was numb, still shocked at what horrors he and his neighbours had observed and worrying if his neighbour had phoned the Old Bill. It took him an hour to stop the nervous tics and the flashbacks and just as he was coming back to normality, they stopped at Wetherby Services to pick up John. After a few cans in the car they all needed the toilet. Tony came into the toilets to wash his face and hands as Gus had been sitting on his knee and offering him ham and pease pudding stotties, which he declined, because he definitely hadn't washed his hands after the flower bed incident. He still felt he needed a wash. They entered the toilet to the sound of massive explosions coming from the one locked cubicle and an awful smell emanating through the gap in the doors. Tony's face twisted in pain and disgust, obviously traumatised from a flashback to his garden and the remains of last night's curry incident.

Gus stared at the closed door, sniffed his nose and, seemingly recognising the emissions, smiled and said: 'That thoo, John?'

A voice came through the toilet door and toxic gasses: 'Aye, it's me. Hope you've not drunk arl the beer yet you ginger twat?'

Tony looked around at his travelling companions all of whom were uninterested and seemingly accepted that the sounds and smells must have been their mate. He said to Gus: 'How did you know that was yr mate. There's hundreds milling around here?'

'It's easy man. We'd kna that arse anywhere. He's worse than me and you're in for treat once the beers get into him.'

And sadly for Tony on the return home he was.

Sunderland were beaten of course, the first of the next seven defeats Marc would experience at Wembley. The day had been the usual - get up happy, get happily pissed and go to the match happy, then come home manically depressed in the car for hours. In between they had visited John's Auntie and she had given them pork pies from the freezer. Gus and John ate them frozen. No one else would. She also gave them ham and pease pudding sandwiches, which everyone but Marc ate. Marc was too nervous and the tablets weren't working as well as normal he believed. His tortured mind reconciled this because he had failed to get his ritual match day cornflakes or his egg, bacon and tinned tomatoes. The omens weren't good.

On the tube to Wembley from where they'd parked the car, they met the first Norwich fans. It was obvious they had never met the likes of the hordes of lunatics down from the North East as they looked worried and nervous. Gus decided he had to take the piss somehow and sure enough he spotted a lad wearing a woollen shaggy jumper. Its colours were gold and green - Norwich's. Gus swaying with the drink pushed past people on the tube to confront the six lads standing holding onto the overhead rails. 'How man: yeah lads arlreet?' he stammered with his face in theirs.

'Pardon mate?' one of the Norwich lads asked, Durham pitmatic language lost on the boys from the carrot fields.

'You'se arlreet man?' Gus repeated. And he continued despite no acknowledgement of his question. 'Thoo's got a canny jumper there mate.'

The man with the jumper must have understood *jumper* and he replied:

'Yes thank you. My mother knitted it for me before she died.'

'She must have had nee knitting needles man. Did she use a claaar hammer to knit it?'

'Sorry? A what? A clah hammer?'

'Aye a claaar hammer man. For ****'s sake you country boys are thick.'

John pushed in and grabbed his friend's arm dragging him away.

'Howay man Gus, we're jumping off next stop man,' and turning to the Norwich lads. 'Sorry lads, divn't worry he's trying to be friendly but he's a bit leet in the heed on the drink.'

As they pushed back to where the door was John heard the man with the jumper knitted by his loving mother say to his mate: 'I never understood a word those two Northern bastards said. And they call us thick.'

The journey back home was torturous. Marc had relapsed into catatonic depression unable to speak or drink and staring ahead in the front seat at the miles and miles of motorway to go. Keith was driving half-pissed again. Three bodies were squeezed on the back seat with two others sitting/lying on knees. Tony was jammed into the side, John sat next to him and squeezing him with his massive rear end and frame. Ginger Gus was sat on Tony's lap. Both were drinking heavily to kill the pain of defeat. *And why the hell not?* you may well ask. Surely it was better than the verge of madness that Marc was on?

The first flatulence began about Watford. It was John. And it was horrible. The result of forty-eight hours drinking and eating curry, frozen pork pies. ham and pease pudding and burgers and onions. Tony cockled and was nearly sick. The next wind was about at Hemel Hemstead. John let loose a silent one which was more toxic than the first.

Tony spoke for the first time, clearly distressed yet again: 'Come on John, that's horrible. I'm feeling sick man. This is awful. I can't move or breath. You're squashing me and Gus's arse is jammed into my bollocks making me want to piss myself. How long have we got to go with all this man?'

John took another drink of his can, and rubbed his sore head, oblivious to the posh person's problems. Keith shouted back from the driver's seat trying to give his possible new boss some comfort: 'Only about five hours to go Tony. We're nearly there mate.'

Tony stared at the back of Gus's ginger head. The sickness wasn't going away.

Fifteen minutes later, south of Luton John let loose again – silent, but deadly, and a poison gas level about that of pure hydrogen sulphide.

Gus burst into laughter. 'Brilliant John. Brilliant. My arse is rumbling too but I canna squeeze it out yit.'

Tony tried to get a paper handkerchief out of his pocket to be sick in but couldn't get his hands free from the double squeezing of John's large backside and body and Gus's bony arse.

'Come on man. Stop that please. I'm feeling like...'

Gus laughed and shouted out: 'Brilliant John, I think I've pissed mesel laughing.'

'Oh no! No...please not on my leg. You dirty bugger. Can you not stop it man,' Tony wailed. And he shouted to Keith: 'Stop the car, I want to get out! I need to be sick.'

Marc spoke for the first time since the final whistle, staring menacingly straight ahead but oblivious to the cars' back lights accelerating up the M1. 'You can **** right off. The lads have gotten beat and I'm ganning yaem. Yeah winging on like our lass. This car's ganning yaem.'

Keith took no notice of the pleas of his potential boss and carried on driving. Marc was at the psychotic stage.

Gus wriggled his backside into Tony's legs and groin and put in his two pennies worth: 'Ah canna beat your arse John. You're the best, but ah think I'm brewing them up now.' And he tensioned his calves and pushed his hands on Tony's legs and lifted his backside up an inch or so and blew off a huge loud fart onto the poor man's legs and groin.

Tony swore for the first time: 'You absolute bastard; stop it; stop it; stop it; both of you. Just ******* stop it. It's not funny.'

All the lads in the car, except Marc who had drifted off to the land of worrying about the next home match, laughed and Keith said: 'Well, it is a bit funny mate.'

John nudged his distraught neighbour and told him a profound thing which he hoped would cheer him up. 'It's a sad arse that never rejoices.'

'Oh just ***** off!' was all he got in thanks for his sagacious philosophy.

Twenty minutes later as they approached Newport Pagnell, just to prove the idiom he had quoted, John let fly again. This time it ripped the air and with it the pungent aroma which was the trademark of John's arse. This time Tony was sick. Young Keith being kind had given him his pompom hat just in case. After his emesis into the hat poor Tony wailed: 'I need to get some air. Stop this car and let me out.'

Keith who could do nothing because Marc broke his mania and silence again: 'If you stop this car mate I'll bury yeh. We're ganning yeam. The lads have been beaten man and alrl yeh gan on about is that daft twat's arse. It is ******evil - arlways is - arlways was...and that ginger twat is just horrible. Just get ower it and shut the **** up.'

At Watford Gap Ginger Gus lifted his backside again and poor Tony, who had suffered for long enough, finally broke down. It was unfortunate to see a grown man crying and no one really wanted that. But despite his captive's emotion and very real trauma, Gus carried on squeezing them out onto the disturbed lad's leg for some time more. I was told it was well past Sheffield, until he had exhausted the supply of gas. Gus never had any mercy - none.

Surprisingly, Owld Keith never got his promotion either. Nor did Tony ever turn up at a game again.

No one cared.

Weekend and days out at Wembley were always tainted by the result but days at Blackpool were infinitely more fun. Well they were when we were young and single. I left the story some pages back with Davey, John and Depressive Mick on the way to Blackpool after the Villa game. They no doubt enjoyed what was left of the weekend there despite the miserable end of season result again. Daft Billy and his mate Jeff also enjoyed a weekend there before a match at Bolton but as we shall see things went badly wrong in the amorous *Kiss me quick* stakes before the match – as they almost always did for poor Daft Bill.

CHAPTER EIGHT
Blackpool, The Sunderland Skin & Trimdon

Trips to Blackpool were always fun for all teams; even if the football was desperate. Blackpool was special and that is why thousands of people look forward to a Blackpool fixture or anywhere in the North West close by where a stopover weekend in Blackpool is the bonus. Happy days at Preston North End, Burnley, and Liverpool and now of course, as the misery has moved across the decades, Fleetwood Town or Accrington Stanley. Who the hell would have thought fans would look forward to a trip to play Fleetwood? Well, many do, the poor buggers because Blackpool has its compensations.

Post-match Blackpool had all the things that could help cheer one up after yet another particularly difficult result or maybe after a small altercation with Blackpool fans, supported by other North West fans, particularly of Man Utd, who travelled there just for the bother. However, the simple pleasures of the Golden Mile or that temple of all *Strictly Come Dancing* fans, The Tower Ballroom, were lost on Daft Billy and Jeff, his more normal mate the weekend that Sunderland were playing Bolton on Bank Holiday Monday and the two intrepid supporters decided to camp out in Blackpool for the weekend before the match. Much more enjoyable were the pleasures of *Yates' Wine Lodge* and passion underneath the pier with a *Kiss me Quick-* hatted female reveller than the football they expected to see.

They had arrived early evening on the Friday and Billy and Jeff got talking to two girls in a tent next to them who seemed to be up for a bit of a fun weekend. The ladies told the boys if they fancied a drink after they had both been into the town then they were up for it and offered an incentive the lads didn't really need, a bottle or two in the tent.

Billy and Jeff were bent on having a night in town so they immediately went out into Blackpool. After several Australian white wine and hot waters in the Yates Wine lodge and a crawl along the pubs with a failed attempt to get into a nightclub, Billy and Jeff decided to head back to the campsite, frustrated with their unsuccessful wooing. As they got near they heard noises in the girls' tent. Thinking they were awake Jeff, went over and whispered into the closed tent flaps. He must have received a positive welcome as he waved to Billy who watched him crawl inside.

Desperate to empty his bladder, Billy found himself urinating against a couple's caravan and got an earful from some irate Scotsman who heard him and pulled open the caravan door: 'Away tae **** with yeah, afor aye hoy the heed on yeah. Yeah drunken baastad!'

Billy having already felt the wrath of some mad Celtic supporters with fireman's axes at a *friendly* match zipped up quickly and excitedly strolled towards the tent. He could hear the voices of his mate and one of the girls. He crawled carefully into the small two person tent and even though it was pitch dark he could sense two bodies clearly in the throes of early attempts of passion so he squeezed into the tight space to the right and felt the body of the other girl. Wriggling along the tent wall brought him alongside the body, and he whispered: 'Hi pet. It's me Billy. Let me crawl in and keep you warm.'

In the darkness he put one arm over the girl and started feeling and stroking her .'Do you like this pet? I'm Billy, is it ok?' he whispered, as he explored under the blanket. He was getting very horny as he could plainly hear his mate Jeff and his partner some way down the line from where he was in the loving stakes. But he was also getting confused because the girl was not reacting at all to his wooing and making no sound at all. Nor could he feel anything that resembled the parts of the female he was desperately searching for. He carried on moving his hand and squeezing his body under the blanket and rubbing his *urge* against what he thought must be her jeans.

Bloody lass, why doesn't she react or say something, he thought. *This is no bloody fun.*

His eyes slowly became accustomed to the dark and he could now dimly see as well as hear his friend and his partner on the other side of the tent *at grips.*

Why isn't this girl showing some passion or kicking me out, he thought.

And then he noticed the top half of the body had strings and zips hanging off it and no obvious hair or face. He threw the blanket off and could see in the gloom that he was trying to make love to two rucksacks.

'For God's sake! Where's the lass gone Jeff?' he cried out as he attempted to jump up and pull his trousers up. As he forced his body and pants up he clumsily entangled himself in the roof of the small tent which thrust upwards pulling all the tent pegs out and collapsing the tent round all the occupants. All three bodies ended up rolling around inside the collapsed tent, the special moment lost for Jeff and his amorous partner.

The two boys were thrown out.

Jeff's passion ended. Billy's never began.

'Where the hell was the other lass man?' Billy wailed.

Jeff laughed: 'I asked for yeh when I got in and she said she'd met a lad at the campsite pub and went to his tent.'

'Why didn't yeh tell me - you twat,' cried a distraught and very frustrated Billy.

'Thowt nee one would be as daft as to try to shag a rucksack. But heh, Billy, ah was wrang. Ha. Ha. Ha.'

Billy thought that must be the end of his misfortune but he was wrong.

The next day and night they went out again. Jeff had driven into town with his new car and they were leaving it there and picking it up next day. Billy meets a lovely girl and they get on like a house on fire. The girl tells him that she's sharing a room so maybe they should head under the pier for some real fun. Billy thinks *bugger that*. There'll be the cast of Ben Hur shagging under there this time of night and after last night, he wanted no surprises. He has a brainwave. *Why not use the car?* Great idea: So he borrows Jeff's car keys. Problem is the car is parked in a main street with people walking past. But a young man's needs must and the girl didn't seem bothered at all. So in his lust and desperation they jump into the back seat trying to ignore the people walking past and gets down to his wooing. The girl seems ambivalent to his approaches and lets him get on with his foreplay without any emotion and he starts to think *Maybe that rucksack was a better bet than this cold fish.* Anyway he pursues it and she seems to be getting more into the mood. He thinks, *Happy days are here* but it seems her agitation and squirming wasn't a result of his tender affections.

'I need a wee desperately,' she panted. 'I can't hold it in.'

'For God's sake woman! Can't yeah just wait? This'll not tak long pet, howld it in man,' moaned Billy, confident in his sexual prowess and staying power after the frustrations of the previous night.

'No I can't and I'm not going out there. It's a long street and nowhere to hide. I'll have to wee in here.'

Charming, Billy thought *I dee pick 'em.*

'You can't piss in here man, it's my mates new car. He'll knack me.'

'I have to!' the poor girl wails.

Billy thinks on his feet. *Is there a used can of beer or bottle anywhere?* And he searches and finds nothing. All he finds is the thin plastic cover that surrounded Jeff's new shirt from *Burtons the Tailor* he'd bought for the weekend. *Champion, maybe she can piss into this?* And he suggests it.

The girl's delighted and takes her pants down and squats on the back seat with the bag under her. As she sighs in pleasure, Billy screams in pain: 'For God's sake stop! It's pissing out of the holes in the bag man.'

'I can't stop you bloody idiot!'

And she didn't. All over Jeff's new back seat.

For those of you who remember buying dress shirts, they always had air breathing holes in them for child safety. They were not meant to serve as portable toilets. Billy looked at the urine stained seat and shook his head - he'd worry about Jeff later. He had more pressing matters on his mind. He was still rampant. His new girlfriend seemed to be too as she sighed:

'That's better. Let's get on with it then.'

And she stretched out on the seat trying to avoid the wet patch. *Romantic types lasses were those days* you might well say. Well, she was from Burnley and this was Blackpool and what happens in Blackpool should stay in Blackpool.

Billy was eagerly hoping he might consummate this passionate relationship when the girl sits bolt upright.

She whispered loudly, looking frightened: 'It's him! It's my boyfriend. I thought I'd seen him go past a few minutes ago.'

Billy looked out of the car window into the street and could see through the steamy window a few shapes walking but it was after all a main street and he'd seen lots of them.

'What the hell are you deeing with me then if you're here with yeh boyfriend?'

'I'm not with him. I fell out with him. We had a row and I came with my mates just to upset him. He must have followed me.'

Oh for God's sake Billy thought. *That's all I need now. Does this misery ever end?*

His paramour continued pouring woe on his head: 'He's mental mind. Jealous as hell of everyone I meet. It's not as if I'm a tart or anything.'

Billy looked at the urine, the bag and the lass lying with her best assets on show to all who cared to look in and wondered about that. She started getting herself dressed and then she about finished Billy's ardour off completely.

'Last bloke he caught me with he put in hospital. Oh shit, look that's him now, get your head down!'

Billy looked out of the front screen and saw a huge, shaven-headed monster approaching, scanning his gimlet eyes and furrowed brow at all the couples and happy bunches of joy makers walking along the Blackpool streets. Billy's head hummed; *bloody hell, he's massive as well as mental,* and he threw himself down onto the half bag of urine and the soaked floor while she buried her head into the back seat.

The apparition passed and they struggled up.

'Thank Christ, he never saw us,' the girl said. She wriggled her small backside sexily onto Billy's legs and said, 'Best not do it here with him searching for me eh? Let's go back now to my mate's bedroom, she might let us jump in bed with her. It's safer.'

Billy, because his brains were in his pants, actually sat thinking about the offer for a moment or two, but knowing his luck, the girls were probably gay. So wisely, he turned it down and went back to the tent to tell Jeff the bad news about his car.

ARSENAL

This Blackpool episode in his young life came back to haunt Billy in a completely unexpected time and place and he had yet another lucky brush with instant death. He was in *The Harbour View* public house overlooking Roker harbour one evening before an Arsenal match. He been drinking for some hours and was desperate for a wee but the pub was heaving. He had to queue for a while to get into the narrow pub toilet. Eventually he pushes in past the outgoing men and boys and squeezes into a space at a urinal. He was just going, 'Arhhhh...' as you do, his bursting bladder beginning to empty, when the door behind him flew open pushing all and sundry into the urinals and jolting him up against the white porcelain, his interrupted wee splashing down onto his new trainers.

A booming voice behind him announced the person who had caused this heinous crime. 'Outta the way man. Ah'm borsting. Just come from Durham. Been on the bus ******** ages.'

Billy, angry, slipped his old man back into his fly and turned rapidly around to face the man, his right fist clenched. He angrily decided in his red misted mind: *This bastard is going to get one of these.* As he spun around the right hand ready to strike upwards towards a chin and a point about his own height he realised his eyes were at about belly button level and as he kept turning around and looking up at his intended punch target, his eyes kept going up, and up and up...*For *****'s sake, how big is this twat?* pulsed through his mind as the body pushed past him to the next urinal.

'Room for a big un there mate?' the giant asked Billy rhetorically as Billy wisely dropped his clenched fist to his side and zipped up as the huge man squeezed his massive frame into the space between John and another squashed punter. The giant gave some belated apology to them. 'Sorry lads, but ah'm borsting.'

Billy looked up towards the ceiling where the man's head was pushing against and saw the full size and horror of the creature. Its head was the size of a medicine ball but the most curious thing, apart from the acromegaly, was that its fully shaven head was tattooed with full colour large scorpions on either side. *Bloody hell* Billy thought *this guy is easy for the Old Bill to spot. No wonder he'd just come from Durham.'* He left the killing zone and went back to tell his mates of his near miss with death. Unaware that at the next match he'd hear more about this giant and his giant slaying.

EVERTON

Billy was sitting in *The Sappers*, The Royal Engineers Club on Roker Avenue on Saturday before the Everton match with lots of the lads. Manic Marc was there with his Everton mates from Cumbria. There was a tradition that Marc, John, Ginger Gus, Keith etcetera were invited to Goodison Park to watch when Everton played Sunderland and vice versa. Ginger Gus loved the simple Cumbrian folk as he took the piss relentlessly out of them particularly their propensity to engage with sheep and the products that came from them: 'Heh, Don, love your new tank top mate; its mint. Did your mother knit it with a claar hammer?' The ginger one's classic one-liner, followed rapidly with, 'Did you have to shag it to let it give yeh that wool?'

The Cumbrians weren't particularly into the footie styles of the 80's and 90's - Burberry, Stone Island or Aquascutum were brands lost on them. The nearest to Pringle they got was their mothers' claaar hammer, multi-coloured, knitted tank tops. Time and fashion had passed them by and for Ginger Gus this was a constant source of pleasure as were the various body sizes and haircuts of his victims in the club.

He spotted Big Hec and shouted over to large man: 'How man, come ower here yeah fat bastard, Marc'll put a pund in yeah pot.' Gus liked to volunteer his 'mate' to donate to the huge man's charity collecting bucket.

Big Hec, a huge man, six foot eight inches and over twenty stone, was a familiar sight in the pubs and clubs of the Region collecting money for charity. A gentle giant from South Shields who raised over a million pounds for local charities, today he was one more link in the Billy and Blackpool and Scorpion head story and Ginger Gus's next one liner.

Big Hec came over and handed his bucket to the lads for contributions.

Gus grinning through ginger tash kindly asked after the massive man's well being: 'How man Hec. Is thoo arlreet?'

'Wye aye man, nivva been better. What dee yeah think is wrang like?'

'Nowt much, ah thowt yeah might be poorly? The weight's just pouring off yeah man,' explained our sarcastic red haired raconteur.

'Ah'm not on a diet,' Hec replied, unaware of Gus's intended sarcasm.

Oh shit John thought *here we go again; I'll have to stop the ginger jester getting battered again.*

'We can arl see that man,' Gus commented laughing.

'Here Hec, yeah may as well have our domino card money,' Marc shouted, and threw the money into the bucket, avoiding yet another nuclear war caused by the challenged one.

Hec, oblivious to Gus's less than subtle humour, was delighted, thanked all the lads and walked over to the next table.

'Bloody hell that bugger is as big as that bloke our lass and me met on the plane last month. What a monster he was,' piped up Jacko, one of the Everton-supporting, sheep jumper wearing lads. 'We were in Newcastle Airport and it was full of Newcastle shirts and everyone seemed pissed when they boarded the plane to Benidorm. We had seats about half way down and not long after takeoff four lads at the back were riotous, pissed, swearing and singing footie songs. A father turned around and asked them to keep the swearing down as he was with his wife and two kids and it was upsetting them. Then one of them stood up and just nutted the man. The stewardess went running down and he lamped her. Next thing we know another stewardess and I suppose the other male pilot are coming down the aisle with some sort of restraining cuffs. I thought this isn't going to go down well. They got about six rows in front of us when this huge arm just stuck out, stopping them in their tracks and then the biggest bloke I've ever seen stood up. His head couldn't fit in the cabin. He turned around, his back stopping any of the stewards, and he said to them: *You stay here. I'll sort them oot.*

'He strolled down the cabin and hurtled into the four lads. One by one he knocked them all out - their mates just cowered. We had to land at Birmingham and the Old Bill came on to arrest them. Two were stretched off still unconscious. The huge bloke was treated like a hero, free drinks and clapping all the way.'

Jacko took a drink of his beer as everyone revelled in the fact that their rivals had ended up hors de combat but Jacko wasn't finished: 'You know what? It wasn't that he was so big that terrified me. It was the two huge scorpions tattooed on his bald head. Who the hell does that?'

Billy nearly spat his beer out: 'I know that bugger. He's a lads' fan.'

And indeed he was. A few years later while trawling RTG, the Sunderland Message Board, John spotted a thread about *The Sunderland Skin* who was the character in *The Far Corner* book that Harry Pearson and his wife had had been terrified of - a huge monster that prowled the streets of Harry's town on the Tyne. *Dear God, he has no neck,* his wife's exclamation when Harry pushed her into the car as his huge nemesis approached him.

On reading the *A Love Supreme* Sunderland Message Board thread about this apparition, and always having been curious about who actually *The Sunderland Skin* in the book was, John was finally enlightened and reconciled to Harry's story of the huge man. It appears *The Sunderland Skin* could well be a real person with two huge scorpions tattooed to his head. On this evidence he could have been both Harry and Billy's nemesis and on the balance of probabilities could also even have been the drunken imbeciles' grim reaper on Jacko's plane. Proof dear reader that many things you may read in this wonderful book may stretch your understanding of reality with more than a hint of truth. In this universe, these are people you'd only think to meet in Dante's Divine Comedy.

After hearing Jacko's story, Billy told them all the toilet episode with *The Sunderland Skinhead* and his back seat of the car horrors hiding from the Blackpool Skinhead.

Jacko listened intently because he had another relevant lunatic story and was desperate to share it. 'When we arrived on holiday after that flight from hell, we were plagued day in day out with timeshare salesmen. Every morning they grabbed us as we came out the hotel to the beach. Then the next week this family arrived. He was built a bit like that Big Hec bloke but not as much bulk, long, thin and muscled, wearing a string vest type thing and baggy shorts - tattoos all over. He looked a bit like a body-built Jimmy Nail. He strode in from the doors and walked straight to reception and asked: *Where's the bar?* When he was told there was one at the pool he strode out towards his personal oasis for liquid refreshment. His wife came through the hotel door dragging two small kids, a chubby boy and thin daughter, and carrying two suitcases and hand luggage. My wife was livid: *That bloody man, straight to the bar and leaves his wife and kids to carry everything. What a horrible human being.'*

Jacko looked at his audience for sympathy with his wife's angst but as none seemed perturbed by the actions of this father. That worried him a bit, but he continued: 'Anyway that evening I could see them around the bar. He was pissed and she was looking after the kids. My wife was even more furious. I stood next to him in the buffet queue for dinner and asked him where he was from. He told me a place called Tri… Trim….Trimdon?'

Jacko was curious to know if his new mates were aware of the place. His local audience smiled and nodded in their understanding.

'They eat their young out there mate. Trimdon, Esh Winning or Shiney Row. It disn't matter. It's life, but not as you will know it mate,' Ginger Gus explained.

Jacko looked worried but continued: ' Anyway, the next morning we were sitting in reception getting the courage up to face the timeshare sales people when matey and his family come down. He's striding ahead empty-handed and she's carrying all the beach towels, bags, inflatables and water bottles. The kids had bucket and spades. He bursts through the door into the sunshine followed by his family. *This should be fun,* I said to my wife. *Let's go see what he makes of the salespeople.* And sure enough they pounce on him as he bounds out. Then his wife and kids arrive behind and the woman in the team collars the wife and a man takes the daughter and begins to lead her away to give her a drink and some sweets from the table set up with refreshments for their potential customers. *Oh dear,* I said to my wife. *Don't touch the kid man. This isn't gonna end well my dear.* The lunatic sees the man grab his daughter and he does no more than headbutts the man in front of him, steps over the fallen body and thumps the man with his daughter, knocking him right over the table of drinks which scattered all over the street. The two other timeshare men ran headlong down the street. He takes his daughter by the hand and gives her to his wife and steps over the unconscious bodies, calling after his dear ones who looked uninterested at the salespersons' fate as if this was a normal day in Trimdon Junior School: *Haway man, hurry up, we're on holiday.'*

'And he strode off oblivious to the dead bodies on the pavement.'

The lads chuckled at this episode and Jacko's face beamed as he explained the aftermath: 'We never saw the timeshare people again that week. Even my wife bought the crazy man a drink along with all of us in the hotel. Mind you, he never left the bar after that one day at the beach.'

'Billy did you ever manage to get a lass into bed at your Blackpool trip, mate?' John asked changing the subject back to Billy's story.

'Nah, nee luck after that second night horror story and the Bolton match was desperate as well. We'd been on the Australian white wine and hot water all weekend and I was caught short at the ground. Had to bring my dirty pants out of the bogs in a bag, left them at a crash barrier and forgot them.'

Marc astonished, piped up: 'So that was yeh! We stood next to them. You couldn't mek it up. I thowt it was John's arse at forst but a gadgy standing with his wife and two kids on the steps three above, who were holding their noses clearly in pain, shouted down to me: *It's not him man. Look down on the stanchion man. Some dirty bastard has left his filthy underpants there in a plastic bag. We moved up here from there. They're horrible.'*

Billy looked sheepish. Indeed, the match and Blackpool had not gone well for our Billy with the shirt bag in the car, the sex with a rucksack and the hot Australian white wine underpants.

It never really did get much better with Billy and football trips.

CHAPTER NINE
Manchester United, Tommy Ducks, Geordies & York

Trips to Blackpool were much easier from Manchester and when Mick and John studied at Manchester University they could attend many matches around the North West and watch either of their two teams. Always in Manchester there would be what you might call, noisy neighbour frolics.

Paul was staying with John and Mick when Newcastle played Man United on a Wednesday night. Paul was a Newcastle fan, as was Mick and yet again they persuaded John to go along to Old Trafford with a lad they lived with called the Gargoyle, so named because that was what he was – a gargoyle. He was short, hump-backed and had a long twisted face with a massive head covered with coarse wire hair which he never washed in all the time they knew him. 'Urgh…I don't need to wash - it has natural oils,' his charming excuse. Also he never ever slept. Anytime during the night, he was awake and sat on the bed in a Buddha like position. He said he didn't need sleep. His eyes bulged like *Marty Feldman* and probably had an overactive thyroid but he would dismiss this with his usual guttural, primeval, *Urgh*. He only had a couple of pairs of white (well, grey-stained) baggy underpants and the dirty pair he used to store at the base of his bed. And always, every minute of the day, he was listening to the seventies hit song of the time, *Where Do You Go to My Lovely,* by Peter SarstedtIt was on his record player constantly, day or night.

The guy whose bedroom was next door to him hated him with a passion and he had taken to recording him at the toilet. He told Mick that the sounds emanating from in there were inhuman and not of this world and went on for hours. So he taped the sounds emanating from the locked bathroom door one early morning and played them back. The memory haunts Mick to this day. Joyfully, the tragic end of Peter Sarstedt and that song was a moment of great joy to all inhabitants of that student house. It began when Stan came to visit.

Stan came down with Davey for a Newcastle match. He was by then the alter ego of Sid Vicious of Sex Pistols. In the middle of the night, at about 3 am in Mick's bedroom where everyone was kipping all you could hear were the constant sounds of *Where Do You Go to My Lovely*. Mick told Stan that this had tormented everyone for months. Stan said, *No more* and walked out the room and down the stairs. All that was then heard was the teeth-clenching screech of a needle being scratched across the record and then perfect silence. Stan came back upstairs and explained. He had walked in and seen the horrible sight of the Gargoyle sat on the bed in his Buddha position, naked except for his grey baggy underpants, his red bulging eyes staring intensely at him. He had crossed over to the record player, crashed the needle arm across the record, took the disc off the turntable and threw it out of the third floor window into the main street below. He did all this in silence, turned around and came back upstairs. The Gargoyle sat mortified and gargled out his horror – *Urgh* - but so ended the nightly Peter Sarsted torture

But the Gargoyle was of some use – he had a gun.

It was a Beretta handgun with a magazine full of real bullets. However, the firing pin had been filed down and they decided to take it to the match. Why they did that no one can recall even now in the gloom of senility. Maybe there's some of Crazy Jim in all of us; now there's a scary thought!

They avoided any trouble going there and also the usual mayhem leaving the ground and managed to get onto a double-decker bus towards Oxford Road. Paul had worn a Newcastle shirt under his leather bomber jacket but as the top deck was quite empty he unzipped his jacket. Then at the next stop onto the bus came about eight or nine Man U and they all came upstairs. They saw Paul's shirt and started stalking slowly towards them. One of them was laughing: 'You Geordie bastards are gonna get a good kicking.'

Paul stood up and pulled out the gun, pointed it at them and took aim. They stopped in their tracks and backtracked stumbling and falling in the narrow corridor and down the stairs. Paul then decided to pull the trigger. Of course nothing happened and the last couple who noticed turned back around and shouted to their mates: 'Let's get the bastards, it's a dummy.'

Oh shit here we go John thought but then realised that he had the magazine in his pocket. Why he'd split it from the gun was lost on him but he quickly threw it to Paul:

'It disn't work without the bullets!' he shouted to the first one coming down the bus as confidently and calmly as his beating heart would let him.

Paul, who was serving in the Paras, slammed the magazine like someone in a *Die Hard* movie, knelt in the firing position acquired from his army training and aimed it, calmly as he could shouting: 'Come on you bastards. I'll tak the forst six of youse out.'

The Mancs scrambled for the stairs stumbling down them and made the driver stop so they could jump off. The gunmen managed to persuade the driver they were a threatened species and needed to get to the next few bus stops along. Another kicking avoided.

Manchester United fans can sometimes be arrogant, probably because they have actually won things. But the year they were relegated into the Second Division by Manchester City and, worse than could be imagined, by a Denis Law back-heel, their arrogance was stunted even if their fans weren't. John took Mick and Davey along to watch Man Utd play Sunderland at Old Trafford in what turned out to be a momentous day. There was a huge crowd, thousands of travelling supporters and the usual hell on at the ground and around. Nothing changed much while Mick and John stayed in Manchester - there was always trouble at Old Trafford and around town. At that first Sunderland match, they had to fight their way out of the Scoreboard End into the paddock where most of Sunderland were, Davey and Mick moaning why they were tempting serious harm just watching bloody Sunderland.

'It's character building,' John reminded them as he got hit yet again with a sharpened coin. He stood next to his ex-school mate Terry, who had been collecting the coins which had been showering him for some time from the Man Utd nutters.

'That's three pints I've got now,' Terry said smiling, counting his coins. And sure enough sometime later in the safety of a

Fallowfield pub after Sunderland managed to lose a really exciting game 3-2 to a Sammy McIlroy late goal, Terry was drinking his *earnings* kindly donated by the winning fans.

'Did I tell yeh about the Man U fan that was standing next to me at Roker Park one day?' he asked John, Davey and Mick. They shook their heads, a few sharpened coins falling out of their long hair. 'This guy was waxing on about his club. I told him to look at the pitch at Roker. It's the best in the league. Beautiful Cumbrian turf and never changes winter or summer, unlike shit holes like the Baseball ground. I said his team should be proud to play on that.'

'*At Old Trafford we walk on water,* was his scornful reply. *The twat;* so I told him: *Can you not piss in the nyueks* like decent people dee?'* (*nyueks are toilets)

Yes, Man Utd fans could be arrogant - and were often destructive on their Second Division travels. Don't think they ever understood what had brought them sp low.

YORK

Sunderland seemed to travel the following week or soon after to all the clubs that Man Utd had played on their away matches that season. It seemed Man Utd had a mission to invade and take every town in the Second Division.

On the Sunderland York trip the supporters were lucky as Man Utd hadn't been there yet and the day had started well. It was John's 19th birthday and as a treat Manic Marc had bought him a twenty-four half bottle crate of *Federation Special* for his present. They started drinking in the Gardener's CIU club at 8 am and piled onto the bus at about 9 30, hoping to get into York for opening time. Billy was with them and hoping for a better weekend than his Blackpool one. By the time they got to York everyone was bursting and as the bus pulled over everyone piled out and the hordes lined against the bus for a French style open air wee. The police descended immediately and began arresting people one by one, moving up the line.

'For Christ sake, come on, come on, get out you bugger,' Billy muttered frustratingly at his exposed penis trying to finish his piss which stubbornly after eight pints would not stop flowing. Marc and John finished and ran off just before the police nabbed the guy next to them, leaving their mate to his fate. Billy, twisting his face and squeezing as much as he could, realised that the long arm of the law was about to beat the long arm of the dribble still coming out of his bladder so he had a choice, banged up or wet pants. He chose wet pants and ran after his mates, his Levi's crotch and leg revealing the result of too much *Fed Special* and too little toilet time.

'You bastards could wait,' he wailed to his two dry mates as he caught up panting.

'Stop whinging man. It's kicking off at the bus and those poliss are looking ower at your wet legs you daft bugger. There's a pub here it's heaving but let's push in. You can dry yoursel in the toilet,' Marc said, comforting him as mates do. They legged it into the pub followed by three or four police.

'Let's see if we can get out of the bog, it's gonna gan mental here,' Marc, shouted through the cacophony as more police kept piling in, lifting fans for no reason. The intrepid travellers pushed into the toilet and lowered the sash on the top half the window. Marc climbed out, followed by John and then Billy. Billy squealed in pain as he slid his leading leg across the window latch and down the outside. Marc shouted at him hanging half way in and out of the window: 'Come on you soft twat! The poliss is steaming in. Let's tilt down this back street. There's a pub at the bottom.'

And they started running.

Billy was left struggling to get off the latch and lift his other leg out. He howled out: 'I'm stuck and it's caught me trousers man!'

'Just jump out you soft bugger,' Marc shouted as he jogged down the street, not particularly worried about his mate. It was 11.20 and they'd not had a beer since the bus incident. 'If the old bill catches you or you miss us we'll see you in the pub next to the ground.'

Billy never turned up at the pub down the road. They assumed he'd been lifted by the police but maybe if he was lucky they'd just caution him and let him go. If not, an afternoon in the cells wouldn't harm him again. The lads enjoyed an hour and half there where the landlord was delighted as the fans drank him dry, and unlike Man Utd the previous December, they didn't smash the place up.

'We better head off to another pub as this one's dry and the poliss will be shutting the others I'm sure. Let's get to one next to ground,' said Marc.

Sure enough that pub was heaving but again with a very happy landlord and the police in attendance seemed to be letting the mental cases enjoy their day out. About 2.30 pm the lads had given up on Billy when he pushed through the bar and waved over to where they were squeezed against a stone pillar. As he got nearer and a space appeared next to him, John could see he was limping badly and his jeans were cut and stained brown all down one leg. Concerned he asked him what had happened. His reply made them all laugh out loud at the poor man's misfortune.

'You bastards! You left me hanging there. When the first copper came in the netty I heaved my leg over and fell out of the window. I nearly passed out with the pain. I tried to run after you but was in agony, blood running down me legs. I got around the corner and dropped me kegs and what a fright! My ball sac had been ripped open by the window latch. It was ******** agony.'

'Hah. Hah. Hah,' the whole lot howled, without any sympathy at all for poor Billy's brush with emasculation.

'Where've you been then till now? You might have missed the match man, you daft twat,' Marc asked, seemingly uninterested in his medical distress.

'I went to Accident and Emergency you sad bastard. I sat and waited there looking like a daft twat with me ball sac hanging out and bleeding down me leg. Women were moving their kids away from me and nurses laughing and taking the piss. The doctor who stitched them up was a huge darkie who couldn't speak good English, nivva mind Geordie, and I thought he was gonna chop the f**kers off. Never been so scared in my ******** life.'

The lads kept laughing and laughing. Marc looked worried and ended the joviality as he supped his beer off and handed Billy the glass.

'Get the beers in. Yeh've missed yeah torn lazing around in hospital you tight bastard. Only thorty minutes to kick off.' And turning to his mates, he swallowed another antacid *Rennie*. 'How can you all laugh at this daft twat when the lads are about to play?'

On the club bus on the way back, Billy was tortured by everyone about his testicles apart from Marc who was only interested in one cunningly sliced ball; the one that had won Sunderland the two points on John's birthday. This was of course momentary. By the time the bus left York city walls he had begun worrying about the Manchester United match in two months time.

NORWICH

Not long after Billy's York testicle trauma, Man Utd visited Norwich causing mayhem, with lots more trouble at the League Cup semi-final return leg at Carrow Road in January. When Sunderland arrived after this some bars were closed for fear of yet another horde of Northern thugs descending.

Marc had persuaded two innocent students from his college to drive him and John all the way down and back from Southport. When they hit the first open pub it was heaving. The two innocents were worried as there seemed to be more lunatics per square inch than their Educational Psychology text books had case studies. They were even more astonished when all of them seemed to know their two student travelling companions. The landlord was also worried as he'd had to close his pub in January when Man Utd came down. The police were all over him expecting a similar occurrence today with the cast of Deliverance and Clockwork Orange mingling in his hostelry.

John in his kindness explained to the police and landlord that these people had not evolved yet and were no problem and he told him of that great anthropologist and mystic, Gaddafi, and his thoughts on it all - all they wanted were the basics of life - beer, a widower's pension and a good football team. He comforted the landlord it was best to get more beer in as they will drink more than he'd ever seen. He didn't believe it as Man Utd fans had drunk him dry in three hours. John still advised him to get more drink in.

Jim came over for a beer and was in great spirits as he'd survived an ambush by Norwich fans and as usual had a weird story to tell. Crazy Jim was a treat for the two teacher trainees who had never met the likes of the mercurial man before or, to be honest, ever would again. He and his mates squeezed into the space next to the door. Jim, like John, had grown up strategically placing himself at exits or columns. *Never get yourself trapped or surrounded;* a good maxim for anyone hoping to survive spending your evenings and social life in the vicinity of psychopaths and sociopaths. After the usual greetings and chat about the journey and the pub Jim grinned and explained their small altercation with the Norwich nutters:

'We parked at the University car park. Thought that would be safe spot. But it seems their daft lads know that ignorant away supporters will think the same because almost immediately we were surrounded by them. They were chucking stones and bricks at the car. Collectively we agreed attack is the best form of defence, and besides, 'Mick Of A Thousand Stares' blood was boiling to fever pitch as his nice new car was getting demolished. Not a good thing for anyone in his way when that happened, so I opened the door and he and Paul and Stan ran out at them. Despite they outnumbered us three to one I think, it seems the massive angry redf-aced body with *the thousand stares* and a large hairy *Attila the Hun* looking beast steaming into them with a bicycle chain might have tipped the scales because they legged it.'

'Close shave Jim,' Marc said, in sympathy.

'Aye it was, we were lucky. But the funny thing was when we returned to Mick's damaged car. One lad had remained in it. He was a gay lad who supported the lads and we'd once picked him up to travel with us. He was sat in the back uninterested and reading a magazine. When I climbed in he kept on reading, his head down and calmly asked: *'How'd you get on Jim?'* None of us expected or wanted him to get involved in our frolics. He did what he did at matches - we did what we did. But the real weird thing was that the latest events stimulated Mick to ask me a question that I couldn't really answer. He whispered to me. *'Jim, where did we find this guy?'* And I couldn't give him an answer, as like all of us, I didn't have a clue where we picked him up from.'

Marc and John chuckled and as Jim began telling and chuckling at more tales of the unexpected, their student driver and his mate stared at Jim as if he was a seminar and educational psychology lecture all rolled into one.

The landlord had more booze delivered from his sister's pub. The lads drank him dry of his first lot and the second lot in two hours and didn't smash the pub up. Even the police were impressed with the drinking prowess and friendliness and let his family trawl the town pubs and off-licences for more drink.

'You lads can come back anytime,' the smiling landlord told John and the boys.

'Stuff that mate: We'll beat you'se today and will be in the First Division next year while you're still munching carrots like Bugs Bunny,' Marc said, the drink, the nerves and the passion getting to him as the match approached.

Of course, the match ended 0-0. Norwich along with Man Utd got promoted - Sunderland didn't. And Marc was not eating carrots but humble pie.

The only bonus about Norwich taking Sunderland's rightful place in the First Division was that at least Marc didn't have to travel seven hours back to college the next season from tractor land. His trip back after this match was gruelling and they arrived back just in time to attempt to woo the last girls left at the Saturday night college disco. The student driver and his mate were still shell-shocked from Marc and John parachuting into the Norwich fans from the overheard stanchions in the shared stand and couldn't comprehend the quantity of cans and beer staining their Dad's new car, so they went to bed. Never to be seen at a match again.

'Soft twats; that'll leave maere lasses for us', John said naively to his manic mate. As there were six girls to every man, even these drunken, dishevelled and smelly youths couldn't fail could they?

Well, after eight cans and a *Watney's Party Seven* each in the car and a few vodka and limes at the disco - maybe they did.

Manchester in the seventies was unusual in that Man Utd were not winning anything and Man City were not rich. Both sets of fans still fought each other and John used to watch and support Man City at Maine Road which was always less threatening than Man Utd those days. The main problem living there was that he, Mick and Davey, Paul, Stan and others who came down from the North East to stay with them were all Geordies. The *mackem* thing was not common at all. Anyone with an accent was a Geordie and for Manchester nutters a target and it always seemed to be with Newcastle United that problems arose for John.

The students John and Mick often drank in an infamous bar called *Tommy Ducks*. It was in town and opposite the Midland Hotel in East Street. It was good for a couple of reasons. The first and main one is that you could get a lock in there after the Student Union Bar shut at 3 pm - for the younger reader, these were the days long before the pubs were allowed to open all day. The second reason was it had girls' underwear stuck on the ceilings allegedly put there by grateful female customers.

It also had a coffin in the bar.

Mick and John and their student friends were welcomed in there many times and came to realise that the police drank there as well as more than a few villains. Also the cast of *Coronation Street* imbibed there too and members of the cast had left their knickers on the ceiling. They couldn't get too excited by Ena Sharple's drawers mind!

This Friday, Davey, Phil, Paul, and others had come down from the North East to see John and it happened that the next day Man U was playing Newcastle. Mick brought a Newcastle fan from Ashington that he knew from his hall of residence as well. All was well until John heard a commotion at the end of the bar near the door and shouts of: 'Get the Geordie bastard.'

By the time John got over to the door several lads were piling into the Ashington lad. John jumped in and was hauling one and then another over the tables and two others jumped him and pushed him towards the open door. As he looked up he saw the landlord whom he knew well, and looking into his eyes tried to communicate something of the man's true interest. *Heh mate stop this I'm your best customer,* but the publican dropped eye contact and shouted to his lunatic assassins: 'Get stuck into the Geordie bastard.'

Nice, John thought, *so much for customer loyalty and care and also geography.* The next thing he knew he was tumbling through the door, two lads punching and kicking him with a third trying to pull him down by his hair. They ended up rolling around, and to quote Jonny Cash, *In the mud, the blood and the beer.* One lad fell with him and John had a tight grip of his ears and was nutting and biting him and rolling him into his own mates' kicks aimed at the unfortunate John but battering his aggressor. The trapped assailant heard the police siren and his mates shouting for him to run for it. He pleaded: 'Come on Geordie! Let us up, man. The Old Bill's coming.'

For some unknown insane reason John let go and they both stood up. There were three other lads around obviously his fellow booting tormentors. 'Come on Geordie, let's leg it!' They grabbed his arm and encouraged him to run with them. And crazily, both Mick, who had stood by John and survived the mayhem and John did run - right down a lane and into the back door of a pub the crazies obviously knew as it should have been closed. They went into the bar, all calmed down and began ordering beers.

'Here Geordie get this down you,' one said offering him a pint. John took it gladly and swallowed a large quantity of it.

'We were lucky there mate. Just got away from the Old Bill, last thing we needed today.'

'Why?' Mick naively asked, looking for the nearest exit.

'We got out of Strangeways this morning. Five years for armed robbery,' said the one. This slightly worried John as he was the one whose nose he had half eaten. 'Anyway, that was a canny scrap. You did alright. We enjoyed it. Let's get another one in, makes a change from porridge,' said the biggest shaved-headed nutter. He drank his pint off in one, ordered another round and then said, 'Come on Geordie we're going to book a taxi to Moss Side. After a night with our mates we'll take you to the Nile Club. The owner owes us a favour.'

As the turkey in the Bernard Mathews *Bootiful* Christmas advert said when it saw the first snowflake fall and its Adam's apple rose up and down, John went…*Gulp!*'

Mick adopted his usual forlorn demeanour and whispered, 'I just kna we're deed.'

He whispered to remind John that two weeks before someone had been beaten to death with a baseball bat in the Nile Club and months before two were shot. 'No way are we going there with this lot; once the beer gets worse they'll soon remember who gave them their swollen jaw and the bitten nose.'

John said 'Ok' and went off to the toilet with Mick. They forced the window open and crawled through it. They both were fit those days, and did a runner down down Oxford Road and onto the bus home. That night they all met up again at the Student Union dance and shared war stories and arranged to meet up to go to the match the next day.

It was the usual mayhem afterwards; Paul and John chased by about thirty of them up Warwick Road, after they had followed them for some time. Then the policeman, who they thought might save them when they asked for a little help, just told them: '**** off you Geordie bastards.'

This, as the police knew very well, confirmed to the mob that they were cannon fodder for their Dr Martens. So two young lads were sent to prove the ethnicity of the two victims one last time by asking: 'Heh mate have you got the time?' - the classic attempt to get you to speak and reveal your accent. Being wise to this, the hunted pair who had grown up together as brothers didn't have to think - two well landed punches and a jump over the prostrate bodies as they hurtled into a fast sprint and then leapt into the loving back seat of Davey's Cortina which luckily he'd been driving around looking for his lost friends. He tore through the crowds with the screaming mob booting the car and waving fists at the disappearing rescue vehicle.

Finally, they were safe; yet again another eventful match in Manchester.

After the match bathing their wounds in Student Union's beer, served in that abortion of a vessel, a plastic glass, Davey from

Washington and John headed out to find stronger, better drink and to try to woo the ladies by stealing customers' beer in the Manchester Hofbrauhaus.

Afterwards they went to the world famous Plaza Cafe to enjoy the only meal the owner of doubtful ethnicity, Charlie, served, Chicken Biryani. Of course it all ended with Charlie and his staff chasing them with hatchets as they did a runner without paying. Then, after paying up when surrounded by the cast of Zulu, they strolled off for a stomach pump in the conveniently adjacent Manchester Royal Infirmary. It had been another great day at the football for both rival armies.

CHAPTER TEN
Bury, Bolton, Burnley, Police Romance &
Gambling

BOLTON

As the years of football result misery rolled on Bury, Preston, Burnley, Blackburn, Liverpool, Bolton, Everton were all great days out, from a base in Manchester or back home in the North East. Bolton was always interesting as Andy, one of Marc's best friends from college, had a father who had once captained them and also Scotland. He played with Nat Lofthouse, that Bolton and England stalwart and hero. One day Andy used his influence to book the lads a half of a corporate box in the old wooden stand. John drove down in his company car with all six of them packed into it. Several beers in the pub opposite the ground and the mob piled into the box for free booze and bait with Andy. The box was split between Bolton and Sunderland, but was good fun – well at first.

As kick off approached a debate about football started between the two fans over which team was the most famous and who knew more than the next about their team. Manic Marc loved all of this because he carried his facts in his head and his cuttings in his wallet - plus he was a rabid gambler and cheat. The two tribes decided to have a bet on first goal scored and each put money into the pot. John held the pot. Later as the game ended 0–0, the pot was still there and not won. The most vociferous and arrogant Bolton fan insisted the pot should be waged against who could answer a question about each other's team. He had waxed on all the game about how he was Stat Cat type and knew everything about everything. He threw open a challenge. 'How much is in the pot? I'll double it if one of you can beat my Bolton question.'

John told him there was twenty quid in the pot - he lied; there was ten. The Bolton lad threw in a twenty quid note, clearly drunk and flush with wedge as he had paid for the box for his mates.

'Come on then who is man enough?' he mocked. 'I'll even give you the question.' And grinning profusely he spurted his obviously favourite gambling question out. 'Who scored Bolton's first goal in the 1953 Stanley Matthew's final when they got beat 3-4?'

Marc said he'd have a bash and asked: 'So, if I answer your Bolton question I take the money?'

'Yes. A one off bet on my question if you think you know more about Wanderers than me.'

Marc looked puzzled and shocked and then laughed and said: 'It's been a great day and I'm pissed. Let's have a laugh. Who gives a **** about money eh? Ah'll tell yeah what, if you double the bet a'll tell yeah what his wife and two sons are called.'

The gambler looked at Marc and smiled. His mates urged him on and he gloatingly said: 'Go on then. If you're that pissed and daft enough with you and your mates' money that's your problem.' And he chucked another twenty into the pot.

Marc looked at him and bluffed him again. 'Ah can tell yeah the names of his two grandkids too if you want for another twenty.'

The Bolton man by now was thinking *This can't end well - something's up?* Marc was six foot four and well-built as were John and Keith...and Ginger Gus, was well, mental. The Bolton man had sense. *This bugger must be mental too; best take his money and run.* He finished the betting. 'No, bugger it man. Don't chuck your money away. Come on tell me the names.'

And Marc did.

'It was Willie Moir who scored and if you want to know who the rest are I can tell you but best to hear it from his son.' Marc introduced the Bolton lads to Andy Moir, the great player's youngest son who had sat next to them throughout the match and who had even arranged for Nat Lofthouse to meet them all. Happy days all around, except for one very pissed off Bolton gambler.

The match was the usual nightmare but the beer flowed and the fun. Bolton was unique because it had its own wine, Chateaux Burnden Park. The best thing about it was the label that must have just been stuck on just before they served it as it slid across the bottle and finally fell off when anyone tried to pour some. Only Ginger Gus would drink it – but for Gus it mattered not - he supped all of it.

The most exciting part of the match was the commentator on the Bolton club stream. He was broad Lancashire and more biased than Jimmy Hill, the famous BBC Match of the Day's supposedly neutral football pundit as well as Coventry Chairman. Marc had never forgiven James Hill for his crime when he went onto the tannoy at Coventry and announced to all the players on pitch at the fifteen minute delayed kick off in the Coventry v Bristol City relegation battle that Sunderland had been beaten by Everton. A draw was all that was needed for both teams to stay up, so after Mr Hill's intervention, they passed the ball between themselves for the next fifteen minutes and drew the game. The end result of course was that Sunderland was relegated again and many thousands, like Marc and John, took the lonely depressing journey up North yet again. Nope, never forget *Mr Chin* – it was lovely target, if only...

But that day years later Dave Higson was no Jimmy Hill. He was not posh or rich or with a chin that Desperate Dan would have been proud of - he was just a true Bolton fan. Bolton fans loved him and his catch phrase *Ding dong do*. What the hell is a *ding dong do*? I leave you to find out. I couldn't. Sadly, his commentary on the match was not too politically correct either. As he announced the multi-ethnic teams: '*And number 5 is ugo..ugo..mumbi...erh, ah can't pronounce yer name but 'ave a good un cocker.*'

And the outright bias was, well...biased.

As the ball flew into the Bolton net*: Oh! What a jammy shot; the ball must have hit a divit caused by those dirty tackles from Sunderland.*' And *The lucky, lucky bastard! Jammy Sunderland keeper a scorcher of a shot has just bounced off his hands.*'

He was a legend in his own lifetime bias. Sadly he was taken from the world of real soccer early.

However, that day he was very much alive and well. The lads chuckled at him throughout the dull match, loving the Lancashire craic right up until John collapsed with the drink and couldn't see to drive home. Ginger Gus who could hardly speak suggested he'd drive home, Keith closer to the legal limit decided he better do it. Andy's wife, Christine, came to pick Andy up and was not amused to find him unconscious in the car park wrapped around the lamp post and she cried out to Marc: 'Why did you let him get in this state? How do I get this drunken bugger in the car?'

Marc uninterested at his mate's fate and now worrying about the next match and the stress of getting back in time for Match of the Day slurred in the direction of the distraught woman: 'It's character building, woman.'

And he climbed in the front seat of the car and turned to Ginger Gus, who was slumped over the wheel and mumbled 'Come on you ginger bastard, get in the back. Keith get the car moving. I'll miss the game on telly at this rate.'

Half way up the M6 the lads were pulling into the service station all bursting and dying of the noxious fumes from John's arse again. Keith quipped as he fell out of the packed stinking car: 'If we pick up a hitch hiker, they'll have to be a dwarf to fit in this bugger.'

Ginger Gus rolled out and looked around breathing the fresh, diesel-tasting night air which was preferable to the biological smells in the car, and then, almost as if by intelligent design, a little *Snow White* person came out of the petrol kiosk. Gus couldn't believe his luck. He was in a piss take heaven and delighted. He shouted over: 'How man, is thoo a dwaaarf? Fancy a lift mate?'

'**** off you Geordie ginger twat,' the small person retorted, stuck his finger up at his tormentor and waddled off to his car.

Keith collapsed laughing and then wet himself.

Another fun day out despite the match.

BURY

It was not always misery for the Sunderland lads or indeed for Newcastle during the heady European days. For Sunderland during Peter Reid's era of management many good things happened – the best thing of course was a football team that could actually play exciting football. This was something they'd long waited for. And one day it all paid off. On Wednesday 14th April 1999 at Bury – Sunderland won a promotion match and three days later won the league at Barnsley. It was to be two nights of joy at last.

Bury was a great town and a great club, many days of enjoying the match and the day out – Thwaites Ales a delight. So sad to see how they've ended up. That night in April thousands were descending down and the lads were coming from various places booked into a hotel early afternoon to meet up. John brought a couple of bottles of champagne for the match and they all got drunk in the hotel in the afternoon and the bars in town.

At Gigg Lane, sadly enough for Bury fans, the ground was full on three sides of Sunderland fans and rumours were abounding that there could be trouble. Peter Reid, the Sunderland Manager, announced on the scoreboards and tannoys a request for fans not to invade the pitch and enjoy themselves. And they did.

John smuggled the bottles of champagne and five glasses onto the terraces in the Gigg Lane end of the ground and by the time Kevin Phillips had hit his hat trick the police had given up trying to stop the celebrations. It was time for a drink and John popped the champagne. He poured it out into the glasses and gave them to his mates. He offered glasses to the two astonished Lancashire policemen standing waiting for the crowd to invade. They took the glasses and actually took a small sup with the lads. They must have thought, *What the hell, we can't stop this. Let's enjoy it.* And they all stood amongst the celebrating hordes and drank a toast to finally ending the misery of the Charlton playoff final just one year before.

Super Kev scored four and the game ended with a mass invasion of jubilant and very drunk fans. John dug up a piece of the pitch and planted it in his garden with the piece of the Roker Park he had been given when the builders tore that down. These days that Gigg Lane turf must be worth a lot since Bury have so sadly been forced out of existence. During the gardening on the Gigg Lane pitch they spotted Dinky half way up the floodlights, half-naked, waving his Sunderland shirt, the police trying to talk him down. Daft Billy went over to say maybe he should come down as both of them had to attend work on a Liverpool site tomorrow. The police were shouting up telling him it was very dangerous.

'**** that! Haway the lads...,' he howled out. 'I'm Sunderland, man. This is just like me scaffold - home to me. Haway the lads!'

'Leave me fatha alone you black and white bastards!' And his young un kicked the polis in the shin and tore up yet another Newcastle Match Attax player card and threw it onto the rapidly disappearing pitch. Well he might have done if he was there, but as he wasn't we can only speculate can't we?

The lads stared at Dinky hanging off the floodlight waving his shirt who didn't give a toss so they gave up too. Billy turned and ran back to the celebrating fans and knew his high rise friend would turn up for work safe and sound, or would need bailing out of the slammer. It mattered not; who cared now they'd won!

And he went back on the piss and a happy ending for once.

PRESTON

Not so happy in Preston one Christmas and another poor result and Billy missed the lift home. He'd met a young lady again in the pub and walked her around the block and hoped he might finally allay the jinx that girls and football had on him. His balls had long time healed since the York incident and the terrors of Blackpool were long gone, and he'd had little success with his wooing since. Sadly the girl he had met that night was not up for his more erotic Santa suggestions and he spent far too long trying to persuade her in the freezing cold around the back of the pub. By the time she said she was off for the last bus home he realised he'd missed his own mini bus back. *Bugger it* he thought *I'll try the cop shop and see if they'll let me sleep in there.*

He still had half of his Santa's costume on when he entered the station.

'Bugger off Geordie! We're not the Sally Army. Go there they might take you, and your bloody reindeers. Bugger off before I arrest yeah.'

Billy thought quickly, *Didn't think they'd let me kip here without banging me up on a charge. Maybe I can pull the Inspector card that Marc told me about?*' Marc had stayed at college with a lad whose mother had been the Chief Inspector at Preston station. He'd told Billy that one day they might need that and surely this was that time. 'Haway man: Giz a break. Me mate knows your Chief inspector. That's gotta help man.'

The policeman called his mate over and laughed saying: 'This daft Geordie says he's a mate of our Inspector,' and he turned to Billy chuckling at the clever trap he set the drunken idiot, 'And what's his name then?'

'She is Mary Robinson,' Billy said with a grin and pleaded with an innocent look on his face. 'Come on lads, giz a break, let me kip here.'

The policemen looked at each other and realised he might have some influence, doubtful influence, but why take the chance and they laughed and one said: 'Ok then, kip next door on the bench but you'll be out at 5.30 am when next shift kicks in,' and he lead him into a room with an observation hatch that opened into the main reception desk where he'd first arrived.

Champion Billy thought at least it's warm. *I'll try and hitch a lift tomorrow.*

About an hour later the door opened and young girl with a suitcase arrived with a policeman. 'You can stay here till it's light and then try again dear. We'll ring your sister in the morning in case she's returned,' the policemen said and turning to look at Billy, 'this one's ok but don't let him tell you he's lost his sleigh.'

Billy perked up. At least he'd have company. It seems the girl had lost her job in London and had arrived unexpectedly at her sister's house to stay but her sister was not at home. She had panicked in the dark and cold and thought, like Billy, the best place to help her would be the police. The two chatted and got on together well into the night both not feeling particularly tired.

Billy had the playing cards he carried for gambling games in the pub before the match that day and they sat and played for a while. Then the girl was feeling a bit cold so she cuddled next to Billy and laid her head on his shoulder and he put his arm around her. They tried to doze off in each other's arms. Well, things moved on, and men being men and girls being girls after sometime both were feeling a little excited with the cuddling. The next thing they're on the bench with their clothes half off and Billy trying valiantly to get a position on the bench that worked with his partner. They were trying desperately to get into a 72nd Karma Sutra position when the hatch opened and the policeman butted his head through.

He shouted back into reception to his mate: 'For God's sake get into next door! That dirty Geordie Santa is trying to shag the lass.' And turning back he shouts at Billy: 'Get t'off t'her you dirty bastard. That's it, I've had enough. Both of you get the **** out of my station!'

The other policeman burst in and dragged a poor frustrated Billy from his equally frustrated partner and led them both to the door, and as he kicked Billy up the arse and pushed the girl out into the black frozen night he laughed: 'Dear Lord, we've had bother with you drunken Geordie maniacs before but I've never had one shagging in our station before.'

Poor Billy, yet again foiled at the last minute.

And it got no better for the only place they both could hole up was just that - a coal hole. They went to the girl's sister's house and as she must have been away for the night they got no answer so they opened the coal house and crawled in there in a vain attempt to keep warm. Billy tried to get his frozen partner excited but even the Indians didn't have a Karma Sutra position that could be used on a half a tonne of black coal lumps. The tired and now annoyed young lady declined his attentions with a coal shovel.

BURNLEY

In Len Shackelton's days my father's best friend from work was a man who came from Burnley. He was Uncle Josh, and he lived in Pennywell. These were the days when Pennywell was more like Brooklyn than the Bronx; well it seemed it to me when I used to visit him and his wife Freda and daughters Kathleen and Mavis. Uncle Josh was broad Lancashire, very Catholic in both faith and behaviour. His hair was always Brylcreamed down flat with a centre parting just like all the photos of footballers were in my *Typhoo Tea* football cards and I never saw him in anything other than a three piece suit, tie and bright shiny leather shoes. He and my dad always went off to Burnley to watch the match when Sunderland played. It must have been a wonderful trip for them to get away from the worries of work and family. I always had a soft spot for Burnley because of these links of friendship. It changed once I met their more deranged supporters in later days!

As I was searching the cyber world to confirm the date that Sunderland were relegated from the Championship three years ago I came upon an article in *The Independent* about a trip to Burnley. I am sure my father and Uncle Josh told a similar story but the drink and devil have dulled the memory. If Mr Mckenna could confirm or otherwise if two fully suited-up, hair parted and brylcreamed and with Cockney and Burnley accent between them, were with his father, could you let me know please?

To explain, I quote from the author, Martin Hardy's article in *The Independent* in 2018.

It was, he thinks, approaching the winter of 1957 and a mini-bus full of Sunderland fans were heading back from Burnley when the conditions made driving impossible. Stranded on what was the formative A66, Harry McKenna and his pals knocked on the door of a farmhouse and asked if they could stop until the weather cleared and they could make it home. In return, they offered their labour, so for two days 14 Sunderland fans lived and grafted on a farm, and they never forgot it.

"He loved telling the story," says his son, Dave. "What stuck in my mind, whenever they got back together, was they'd say they'd never eaten so well. He was born in 1932. It was totally fresh produce on the farm. Every time they told the story the ham would get thicker! They loved the memory and they loved following Sunderland."

When he was four years old, Harry McKenna went to see the champions of England, the sixth time Sunderland had achieved the feat. Manchester City's last Sunday was their fifth. Six days later, the gap between the two teams would be even greater.

From stranded on a farm to stranded in the abyss.

Yes, sixty years later Sunderland dropped yet another division to face the abyss in the relentless pursuit of *what good is*. But those days, my father and Uncle Josh had no idea it would get so bad. These were Bank of England days and *Shack* entertained them when he could be motivated to do so. He always was motivated when Arsenal played Sunderland at Highbury and my father loved his days watching it in London.

My father had trialled with Arsenal before the war with Denis Compton, as he had with Middlesex Cricket club, so he had a soft spot for them. Unlike *Shack* who seemingly hated them for rejecting him. My father told me many tales of Len Shackleton, who was the second best player he'd ever seen, the first being Duncan Edwards, his career and life so tragically lost at the Munich airport crash that wiped out so many of the Busby Babes.

It seems *Shack* was what these days we would call a 'temperamental genius' and only played to his undoubted beauty when he felt like it. Shack's behaviour appeared to be like my own when I was told by Brian the Lion one day in Whitburn club when I failed to turn up for the regular Sunday lunch time piss up with him and the most aggressive man I ever met, Mad Jack, that, 'You only turn out when you want to.' Real drinkers, like real footballers, should never miss a session, even if they want to.

My father said that *Shack* always chose Arsenal and Highbury to exhibit his beautiful football skills and also take the piss. It seems every game he destroyed the Arsenal full back or centre back, I can never remember which one now. Whoever he was , he disliked him intensely for being a thug, so he would spin the ball to him using only his pit boot type football boots and wooden studs, watching him lunge at it and then scream insanely as the ball spun all the way back to the waiting *Shack*. Shackleton would either do the same trick again or put his arms on his hips and then sit on the ball. In each scenario *Shack* ended up beating the angry and tormented man by dribbling neatly around a violent tackle and – a bit like George Best in later years - turn around and beat him again. He'd then play up to the crowd. Even Arsenal fans loved it all. Somehow, I just could never see Danny Graham doing that.

Maybe Ginger Gus was related to *Shack* coz he certainly liked to take the piss and not so long ago the lads were at a Burnley v Sunderland match and in the Catholic club next to Turf Moor. They started drinking with some Burnley fans. One was a huge tall guy with a massive gut on him. He had a knitted sleeveless yellow jumper which only reached the belly button, his huge gut and shirt hanging below. He had a purple shirt and a yellow tie with bright ginger hair and blue eyes. His son was with him who unfortunately looked nothing like his erstwhile father and was about five feet five inches tall, thin with jet black hair and brown eyes. Ginger Gus loved him - a gem of a find for the ginger piss-taking merchant. He wound this giant up all afternoon. The half sized woollen jumper as prime target: *'Did your lass knit your jumper with a claar hammer?'* and looking suspiciously at his dwarf son, and his doubtful paternity, and then back at the tall wibbbly wobbly man, he cruelly asked: *'Do you work away a lot mate?'*

The big man clueless to it all answered 'Yes' much to the joy of Gus and to them all. He seemed to take the relentless piss take all in good spirits, or maybe he was just thick - there's a lot of it about.

His mate was even better. He was a small diminutive man with a Burnley knitted jumper and a Burnley woollen hat with a pompom. The Burnley fan's mother had made his pompom hat and jumper in 1964 and he had watched the Claret and Blues man and boy everywhere. But his tales of his traumas at Sheffield and Millwall made everyone howl with laughter.

'I went to Sheffield. I think it was sometime over Christmas. The ground was covered in snow. I had my pompom hat on and was spotted by some of the Sheffield lads. They came across the terraces and I thought I'd get a hiding but they laughed at my hat and took pity on me because I was small. So they rolled me into a gigantic snow ball, with only my little legs and my head and pom pom hat sticking out. Then the bastards rolled me down the terraces. The snowball got bigger and I finally ended up smashing into the wall at the bottom where the kids stood.' He took a drink of his Twaites' ale and finished his sorry tale: 'But they wor nice lads really.'

The whole company chuckled at his laconic tale and Marc asked this lovely placid man if he'd had any more episodes like that.

'A few of course, we all have. But Millwall was hairy. We were on the Tube and on came the nutters. They spotted us and came down. I thought here we go. One came up to me, a huge skinhead, and he pulled my mother's pompom woolly hat off, laughing and showing it to his mates. I was expecting a clout next but I was really lucky. He deliberately stubbed his red hot cigar out on my head and but I was lucky again because he never took my precious hat and he put it back on my burnt head.'

Aye, very lucky indeed, as he showed them the bald patch he still had to that day! His pompom hat and jumper had seen many happy days for sure.

And talk of Millwall and crazed lunatics brings us to Manic Marc, Crazy Jim and other trips to the big city...

CHAPTER ELEVEN
Millwall, West Ham, Fulham & Kippers

Trips to London were always fun. They had changed from my dad's days when he travelled down and enjoyed a few pints with the locals. Very soon it was pints of blood you might be enjoying on trips to West Ham, Millwall, Chelsea and Tottenham. As this is a fun book the horrors of attending matches and strolling along the bloodstained boulevards of Green Street, Cold Blow Lane and Seven Sisters station full of Cockney malice and bumping into jovial fellows like Harry the Dog, Jimmy Gardener and Cass Pennant you can read about on any football message board or the *hoolie* books written about them. But normal people still had to go to these places and they did, so we must tell a few tales of cheeky chappy, diamond geezer, Cockney japes.

Millwall was always special and when Marc and the lads took a Gardener's club bus down, the bricklayers amongst them didn't think they might be put to work rebuilding the slums around the Old Den by the herculean efforts of Sammy the Chin, the hero of the Fulwell end,.

It was a particular challenging game in the stands and around the ground. One Millwall fan attempted to enter the turnstiles alongside the singing raucous Sunderland fans with a fireman's axe strapped to his body, telling the astonished and terrified Sunderland gentleman next to him as he opened his jacket: 'The Norffern ****'s won't be larfing when I start swinging this ****.'

The Sunderland lad informed a policeman who seemed disinterested at first - I guess fireman's axes were like wooden rattles at the Old Den. But his mate, who must have been officer potential and had a brain, gently persuaded the psychopath to move to the Millwall end of the ground. The fact that the axe was kept under his coat and not confiscated, nor the potential assailant arrested, you may find shocking. Outrageous this police negligence for many of you young un's, but this was common in those days before enlightenment in football supporter safety. I guess one should enjoy a match in comradeship rather than be attacked with a chopping axe by deranged cheeky Cockney chappies who thought they were the incarnation of Geronimo or Olaf the Viking. Thankfully, it has changed somewhat.

It seems that Sammy the Chin, a well known *character* from those early days who has recently passed on, had decided to take his own retribution on a Millwall crew after the horrors of the terraces during the match. However, he had come unstuck because Millwall tended to have more psychotic lunatics per square foot of ground than the first few chapters of a Stephen King novel. So sensibly for Sammy, who may well have been the small boy in the first lines of that familiar song below, he made a strategic retreat and found himself running up the stairs of a small block of flats:

When I was just a boy I had no sense.
I bought a flute for fifty pence…

It probably seems a bit daft to you now, running up to somewhere where you can't escape, but heh, Sammy was not known for his mental dexterity. He once climbed up a thirty foot Christmas tree after an away match and toppled it from the fairy position, tumbling with the tree as it crashed into Christmas revellers and rolling to safety paratrooper fashion with sheepskin coat and Doc Martens intact. He promptly vomited into the Nativity set in the window of the local take away - a delightful contribution to the Christmas spirit and Yule tide ambience you may say. Anyway, today he must have been able to get through to the top of the maisonettes and barricade the doors behind the howling mob because he spent the next half hour throwing house bricks down from the roof of the flats onto the baying blue-coloured pitchfork mob. It seems the police were finally called and Sammy escorted safely back to his transport. Michael Caine, Stanley Baker and Ivor Emmanuel at Rorkes Drift had nothing on our Sammy when it comes to surviving incredible odds.

Later that night at a service station on the M1, Manic Marc and the lads were glad that Sammy and his Sheepskin coat had found his way home as he threw a nicely timed brick through the window of the food hall. Why ? No one knew but probably because he could. In the ensuing mayhem Marc and the boys managed to borrow all the pies, sandwiches and also beer that they had just started to serve at service stations. Whether Sammy had saved the brick from the defence of Rokes Drift earlier that evening, no one ever knew as he was locked up yet again.

Marc thanked him at the next match for helping with collecting free snacks. But these snacks were to cause some delay on his usual manic depressive return home as the bus was pulled up by the police some miles further up the M1. He and everyone tried to destroy the evidence as they tucked into cold sausages, sandwiches and bottles of Worthington E. Unfortunately for the Leicestershire police they hadn't seen the trick before of placing the piss bucket on the stairs of the bus, delicately balanced so that if a member of her Majesty's constabulary was to hurriedly demand the door be open and rush in, the piss bucket would tumble and its horrible contents spill onto the neatly pressed blue uniforms. This you may gather didn't please the police but as thirty or so drunken maniacs had devoured the evidence and were spoiling for an argument, the police officers decided the better part of valour was to drive off into the night and a warm shower in the station.

Another happy day at the match Marc reflected as the bus pulled away and turning to John he moaned:

'It's the Mags next week. I'll nivva sleep a wink.'

And he turned to stare manically out of the window and never said another word to his best friend until the bus pulled up in Washington.

WEST HAM

John was to meet his own Harry the Dog some years after this in a bar in Paris. This man had become John's friend over a few months of drinking there and he had named him Whispering Sid purely because he was a bit like Hissing Sid, in that everything he said was in a low key and quiet, as if someone or something was listening or recording the conversation. And indeed, they may have been as he recalled his adventures over many weeks as one of West Ham's original *Inter City Firm*. He was unimpressed with John's tales of past japes and close shaves and the Sammy the Chin bricklaying one he dismissed as 'handbags'. He had grown up with Cas Pennant and the boys in the East End and to him Cas wasn't the hardest. He had been with Billy Gardener when they walked up to the assembled cast of Clockwork Orange in the infamous *Shed End* at Chelsea and Gardener opened up the debate before mayhem erupted, with an introduction that wouldn't have been out of place at the Palace garden party: 'Good afternoon gentlemen. My name is Billy Gardener.'

'Hardest lad I ever met,' was Whispering's opinion of Mr Gardener.

Sid was not impressed with John's war wounds either. The bottle scar on John's forehead did not impress him one bit. And reminiscent of the scene from *Jaws* where Richard Schneider and Robert Shaw trade shark scars with each other, Sid pulled out his USS Indianapolis card. He opened up his shirt and belt and pulled open his trousers and showed John a scar that came up from this thigh, obviously through his underpants and right up into his chest. It seems they had been ambushed by Millwall near the Den one game and one of Millwall gang had decided to open up Sid with a sword.

'We were totally outnumbered and the boys had to get outta there so they threw me over a wall out of the ******'s way and legged it. I rolled towards the ground floor flat of an old lady, bleeding to death it seems. She had seen the ruck outside her window and had phoned the police and ambulance when she saw the state of me. She saved my life that old lady.'

John decided to give up on his own petty scar and war stories as Sid carried on over the weeks telling of serious crime following West Ham and England. He had been banned from many grounds and from all England matches for life and the jails of London were not unknown to him. When Sid showed John two bullet holes from separate incidents which he refused to explain or talk about, John decided better to talk to the West Ham man's new love, Paris rugby. Surely they didn't shoot, garrotte or fillet you there did they?

Sid and John became great friends and John was grateful for his offer to call him, anytime, place or reason if he or his son who was studying in London needed assistance, particularly his and his Cockney acquaintances' unique blend of extreme violence.

As John moved on and grew older and wiser he decided that London matches would better for his health at Fulham, Reading, Brentford and Wimbledon...Sid and his mates' son's still inhabited the old haunts and the ghosts of meat axes, swords and house bricks past still haunt those grounds.

FULHAM

As the years rolled on Fulham became a lovely day out for the lads in London. A great ground to visit and fans that didn't want to dissect and embalm you. And as recently as a couple of years ago thousands made the pyrrhic journey down with Manic Marc, Crazy Jim and the lads to watch Sunderland in the final game of their Championship relegation season. Already relegated by Burton Albion this was just an excuse to have a weekend in London and maybe stop Fulham winning promotion. The match had been changed from the Saturday to a Friday night as Sky assumed that it would be a sell out with Fulham chasing a promotion spot and Sunderland needing to win to stay up and Sky realised it would be great TV. This cocked up many thousands of Sunderland supporters who had already booked hotels and trains for a Saturday kick off. Of course Sky didn't give a toss.

The friends were by now scattered all over the country and the world. Marc came down from the North East, John from the South West, Crazy Jim the South East, Wee Willie from Glasgow, Big Pat from Singapore, Jack from Belgium, Wakey, from well Wakey, and The Ferret, from Thailand. This was a gathering of the clans, Götterdämmerung, the twilight of the Gods, one last throw of the dice before the misery of Division Two and the hope of a final win to cheer up a terrible season. Götterdämmerung, as well as being the final ending of Wagner's Ring Cycle can also mean a situation of world–altering destruction marked by extreme chaos and violence. No one expected chaos and violence at Fulham that day. Nor did anyone want it - everyone just wanted, like many had for forty years, a good football team playing its heart out for the thousands who had travelled from all over the world to watch them win for once. Of course, it never happened.

However, hours before Fulham finally won promotion to the joy of their likeable fans, and total despair of the travelling hordes, the lads had enjoyed many of the delights of London. Big Pat was the huge mate of John with whom he lived and worked with in Asia for ten years. He was the son of an even bigger man who had come from the Durham coal fields to settle as a fisherman in Whitby. Big Pat grew up as a Sunderland fan in a Yorkshire town full of Middlesbrough and Leeds fans. Needless to say he grew up hard; amazing tales of which are found in *A Turkey and One More Easter Egg*, one of my earlier books.

Pat had planned a return to his home town to fall in with the last game of the season and had brought his new wife and son with him for their first trip from their home in Thailand. Prior to this John had sent his son a football strip. As the boy was only three years old he was going to send a 4-5 year old size but wisely decided to check first. Big Pat told him the boy needed a small boys strip 6-7! John should have realised that when the child had been born, nowhere in Thailand had there been bootees or mitts to fit him. The big man had once broken the MRI table that the wonderful Welsh Doc in Singapore had sent him to for a scan. This caused the irascible medic much grief and he expressed it his own inimitable way to John. 'The big bastard is so huge he broke the table. They are going to charge me for it. Why the ***** do I have you lot as patients!'

The good news for John was that Big Pat was bringing some Whitby kippers for him. He used to do this when they had lived in Asia and now he'd promised John a couple of pairs.

They all arranged to meet in a pub on the river at lunchtime where they could take a ferry to Craven Cottage but as it was pissing down they got into a pub near a station that would get them to Fulham Broadway later that afternoon.

John met Wee Willie and Big Pat in the pub. John's wife always made a stone of corned beef pies and a loaf of ham and pease pudding sandwiches for the lads at matches. It was a tradition over the years. Wakey's wife planned all her matches around this. John had these in the rucksack that he always carried them in. After a few hugs and handshakes they settled down to the business of getting drunk enough to endure the torture of watching the match.

Pat said: 'Av'e got yaeah kippers, John,' and he reached under the table and pulled a bin bag out and dropped it on the table.

'What the ****,' John said as he tried to lift the bag, 'how many pairs have you got in here man?'

'Nee idea, just towld them fill it up. They sell 'em by the stone to me fatha.'

John opened the bag and could see about fifteen pairs of kippers. He shook his head as he realised he was going to have to carry these around London all day with a back that was in agony. After a while he thought, *How the hell do I get them in to the match?* But it was early, and the day was young; he'd worry about that when he'd had enough to drink.

Manic Mark arrived. He'd never met Pat and or Wee Willie and he held his hand out to Willie and greeted him. 'Hi Willy, I'm Marc,' and turning to Pat, 'Hi Pat, did you have a canny flight, mate?'

The big man shook his hand with his huge grip and replied: 'Aye.'

'Aye' was the only word most ever got out of the sleeping giant. As Marc and John walked to the bar John was puzzled and asked Marc how had he known who was who.

'For ****'s sake you daft twat. Yeh towld me one's called Wee Willie and is a Jock, and ah see a grizzled little twisty-faced bloke only about five foot two inches high and there is a ******** man mountain the size of that Sunderland Skin that pissed on Billy's new shoes. It wasn't difficult to sus who was who.'

John had to agree, it really wasn't difficult.

The day wore on and Crazy Jim arrived with tickets for some he'd managed to scam by some new scheme he refused to talk about and they all managed to get the sandwiches and pies down but many were left so John offered them around to the other loads of Sunderland supporters they bumped into as they moved from pub to pub. Finally John could stop carrying his rucksack full of bait as well as the bin bag full of kippers because the rucksack was now empty so he squeezed the kippers one by one into the rucksack. It weighed about a stone and was crippling his perpetually knackered back but the drink helped and they headed to Fulham Broadway. A few more drinks and they were walking along the river to the ground.

'How much farther for ****'s sake? I'm bloody crippled man,' John moaned, the kippers beginning to take a toll on his sciatic nerve.

'Only about half a mile; just a jog, I jogged along here few years ago chased by some Chelsea nutters after waving an Irish flag at them with my balaclava and gun,' Crazy Jim chuckled, his dark glasses steaming up in the evening drizzle.

'Half a mile! These bloody kippers will kill me! All I wanted was a couple of pair,' John finally cracked and screamed in the pain of it all.

'Stop whining man, It's nearly kick off and me guts are all over the place and ah canna cope with these black and white strips arl ower the place. It's deeing me heed in man,' Marc droned out riddled with angst at Fulham's colours and in the throes of pre-match nerves.

As they approached the ground it was Wee Willie who first realised that John had to get a stone of kippers through the masses of police and security that were waiting for the hordes from the North and he asked John what was he going to do.

'Nee idea Willie. Guess I'll just walk in. They might not check but after humping them all over London I'm not leaving the bastards now.'

And sure enough as they got through the turnstiles there was a wall of security and police, some with dogs.

'What's in your bag?' the security man standing next to a policeman asked John.

John being pissed and also perhaps hoping for a bit of fun answered: 'A stone of kippers.'

The policeman heard the comment and was not amused. He moved over and intervened. 'Don't take the piss son. Hand the bag to the man.'

John took the bag off his shoulder and gave it to the security man. The policeman let his dog sniff it. The dog went nuts. The policeman said with a huge grin: 'I knew it. You're all the same up there, either pissed or drugged. One more time son, what's in your bag?'

'I told you man, a stone of kippers,' John said, opening his hands in an *I'm innocent guv* gesture.

'Right, no more piss taking off you, you Norvern bastard,' the officer said forcefully and tells the security man to open the bag.

The security man opens the bag to a wiff of Whitby's best which had stewed in a bin bag and then a rucksack for two days. 'What the **** is that smell?' The security man recoiled. The dog is still twisting and turning and whining on the leash like he'd sniffed a stash of raw Charlie.

'I told you a stone of kippers,' John repeated smiling.

The security man holds his nose and delves into the bag and pulls out a kipper by its tail. 'For ****'s sake he's telling the truth. It's full of ******* kippers.'

'What!' exclaimed the other officer in blue and he takes a look in the bag and pulls back his face twisted in pain.

By now they are surrounded by lads who are trying to get past to their seats and getting a bit impatient. 'Leave the lad alone man and let us in!' they shouted.

By now there are a couple more policemen and a couple of security guards around John and his breakfast bag. They look at each other and then at the kipper in the guard's hand and then at John totally bemused.

One of the police breaks the moment. 'What are you carrying a stone of kippers for you daft Norvern bastard?'

John looks at him and said: 'A mate brought them all the way from Singapore for me breakfast.'

The guards and police just shook their heads and the policeman with the dog pulled the whining dog away from the bag and nodded to the security guard to put the kipper back and hand the rucksack to John. As John took it and a gap between the guards opened up he put the bag back on his back and strode through smiling. As he passed the second police officer stopped him by the arm and said: 'Every time you daft bastards come down here there's something new. But a whole haversack full of kippers?

Now, I've never seen that one before.' Then shaking his head he broke into a smile and gave some sound advice: 'Go on now. **** off you crazy Norvern bastard and watch your match. And for God's sake don't open that bag; you'll have our bomb squad and the anti-terrorist mob steaming in. They are all over and on high alert tonight for some reason.'

And then, as if to prove the policemen correct, after the ex-Newcastle player Mitrivić scored the winner for Fulham, Marc finally cracked. With his bald head throbbing red in the gloom of the stands he leapt up and howled at the players: 'You let that black and white bastard score you useless, useless ******** bastards,' and he grabbed the bag and ran a few steps down the stand with it and was trying extract a pair of kippers to throw at his beloved team. John leapt after him and grabbed him. He lead him back gently, trying to calm his tall, red, baldy-headed mate's raging temper and reminded him of the anti-terrorist mob warning. Marc slumped back down in his seat and held his head in his hands and reached for the Gaviscon tablets.

The long walk back along the river, this time everyone miserable, the three tube trains and up and down long flights of stairs, and a half mile walk to his son's flat on the other side of town with a stone of kippers destroying John's back. This trek was becoming more and more to John like the labours of Hercules than a day out at the match. It lead him onto yet another deep internal conflict in his tortured mind. *Why do we do this?* The next day after an early morning long train ride to the West Country and straight into the pub to finally sit down and at last remove the weight of cured herrings off his broken back he asked his mate Marc the same question. 'Marc why the **** do we dee this man at our age?'

Marc being less manic now, the night's game resigned to history was already worrying about next season in the depths of the lower division and simply said:

'It's character building – get the beer in.'

CHAPTER TWELVE
Birmingham, Sheffield Wednesday & Gibbets

'He went down like a bed settee!'

Gaddafi was in good form. His shout that echoed around the Fulwell made many chuckle but like all of his one line chants they were also filled with the pathos of truth that turned many to drink. Gaddafi was like an Iman with his Arab dress and booming hypnotic voice and with his periodic calls to the faithful for prayer. This *bed settee* prayer was for the Sunderland goalkeeper who had not shown much cat-like agility in his ability to dive and stop a pretty tame shot bobbling into the net.

The trip to the ground had been uneventful. The only amusing thing had been that Gus had noticed the metal badge seller had decided to expand his business into taxidermy. The sign enticing the hordes of potential customers to his familiar wooden cross shaped stand had the one word scrawled across the cardboard hoarding advertising his products – *BADGERS*.

It worked! Because it attracted Gus to take the piss out of the unfortunate dyslexic man and John and young Kevin to buy the classic Xenophobic, England, anti-Jorman badge, *WE WIN WARS*.

They don't make them like they used to do.

Indeed, the *badger* man was relentlessly ripped by Gus and young Kevin urging him on which cheered them all up before getting into the game. But the game had not kicked off well at all because Ginger Gus had found a flag before the game in the pub and in his drunken state he was waving it when the match had kicked off.

'Put the flag down or I'll stick it up your ginger arse!' boomed a voice, not unlike Gaddafi's but obviously not so welcoming. Ginger Gus as usual couldn't give a toss if someone was annoyed; in fact it was all the best if they were, so he laughed and carried on waving.

'Ah'l not tell yeah agyen. Put the **** down!'

John decided to see who was a tad displeased with his ginger mate's antics and turned around. There standing as tall as Gaddafi and as well-built, staring menacingly at him, was a young man whose face looked as someone had been using it as a block to chop sticks on and the axe had broken on his face. It was hard as iron and his eyes were grey, cold and silent. *Oh dear John* thought *I've seen this type before, best not try to annoy them.* But this time the face was familiar and then he realised where he'd see it before – in a late night bar in the West End of Newcastle near the train station where he had been drinking with work mates and their mates from Newcastle. These lads were no spring chickens and a few were dangerous people who had done time for serious violent crime, and all were Newcastle supporters. They were enjoying a drink when into the late night bar entered a tall, well-built man with a face that someone had used to chop sticks on. He was drunk and stumbling to the bar had ordered a beer. He then looked around and started calling out the lads in the bar: 'Black and White bastards all of you.'

And jolly tribal bonding greetings like that is all you want as you enjoy a nightcap in the company of Newcastle's version of the Kray brothers.

Obviously it starts to kick off and one or two of the more dangerous lads began to make a move. John spoke quietly to them and said to let him defuse the situation. He went to have word with the agitator. He told him he came from over the water and supported Sunderland but these were friends of his and they were hard men; maybe the gentleman should be a bit more diplomatic and ecumenical with his chit chat? This attempt at reason didn't deter the chopping block face and plainly deranged, he started again.

John stopped it progressing and finally got the maniac one side to talk. As he calmed the man down John found out he was from Seaham. Those of you who knew Seaham before it became the Riviera of the North may understand this could well explain insane behaviour. John knew some of the Seaham lads but he didn't know this one, which again worried him, because God only knows who or what he was. He certainly was not afraid of taking on a bar of mean grizzly dangerous men. The lack of neurones in the cortex and the drink helped of course.

With his undoubted skills at dealing with lunatics, homed over years of growing up with them and managing them, he persuaded the man to drink up and head for his last train which by now had left Central Station. John felt it wouldn't be wise to tell him that bad news as he patted him on his large back and gently pushed him out of the door. He was pleased he'd never see him again and returned to talk with the goodfella's of the Toon.

Now at Roker and in more friendly country, here he was the Seaham psycho again and about to ram a flag pole up Ginger Gus's arse and anyone else with him. Wisely, John had a motivating chat with his ginger friend and took the flag off him. He looked behind and the gorilla scowled at him briefly but his cold shark-like eyes moved back to the utter garbage being enacted out on the pitch. John swallowed with a happy gulp as he realised he hadn't been recognised from the Newcastle incident. This was great news John realised because if the giant had linked his two brain cells he may have produced a synapse of memory recall and identified John as a Mag. Given the flag suppository threat to poor Gus, John was certain that wouldn't have ended well.

Joy overflowing, he never saw the man again until a match in Birmingham where he and two of his more normal friends were being followed by a gang of Birmingham hooligan, Zulu types. They stopped at a corner off licence to get their wits about them and coming out of the shop was *chopping block face man* again with another mega fauna, who looked the spit of him. *Maybe his brother?* John thought, amazed a mother could spawn two of them. The *chopping block man* spotted the gang lurking over the road and growled to the three lads: 'Those brummie bastards been bothering you'se lads?'

'I think they have sussed us mate,' John's mate from Bristol said.

'**** them.' Obviously men of quick decision-making skills and not ones for quantitative risk analysis, they both zipped up their bomber jackets, ran over and steamed into the gang over the road, clattering the first three or four and the rest just legged it, chased by the two horsemen of the apocalypse. John and his mates sensibly let them get on with it and bought a couple of six packs, three cold *Ginster Steak Slices* and headed off to the relative sanity of their car.

Back at the flag waving game, Gaddafi was calling the faithful to evening prayer and Ginger Gus was still miffed about losing his flag but more miffed about the game. He had a thing about goalkeepers and the *bed settee effort* had not helped his angst. And indeed, Gus's knowledge on goalkeepers was legendary. One day he was invited to join on Radio Sheffield for his expert opinion and punditry on goalkeepers.

At Hillsborough in the 4th round of the FA cup Tony Norman the Sunderland keeper had dropped the ball back into the path of Sheffield Wednesday striker Mark Wright to score in the last minutes. The team lost by this one goal and the lads were sat in a car on the way back home, yet again trying to drink through the sorrow and misery. The traffic was terrible and Old Keith was driving and had the radio on to get the traffic alerts. The Radio Sheffield post-match phone-in was on the radio and locals were phoning in about the match. The commentator then asks over the radio what anyone thought of Sunderland's goalkeeper's performance. Ginger Gus perks up: 'Giz the car phone Keith. Ah'll tell the Yorkshire bastards.'

John thought *Oh shit here we go but surely they are not daft enough to have this mad bastard on?* But sure enough they did.

'Hello, I hear we have a Sunderland fan on the line now? What's your name?'

'How man, it's Gus.'

'Ah, good evening Gus. I guess it's a long drive home for you lads?'

'Nah, we're ar'l getting pissed in the car man. Piece of piss travelling to your place.'

'Ha Ha Ha. I hope you're not driving Gus,' the radio man jokingly commented.

'Nah ah'm ower pissed. Keith is driving coz he awnly had eight pints afor the match.'

'Ah well, well...best move on from that. What did you think of your keeper's performance, Gus?'

'The bugger will be hung on a ******** gibbet when he gets back yaem if we had our way. The useless tossa.'

'A gibbet Gus?' the rapidly worried radio man stammered out.

'Aye, dis thoo thick Yorkie twats not kna what a gibbet is man. Arways thowt Yorkshire fowk wor thick and what's more...'

'Well, thank you Gus, and let's move over to Seth from Bramhall...', as the line to Gus was instantly cut.

'That towld them, thick Yorkshire twats,' the ginger one muttered as he pulled the ring on another free can of beer.

MANCHESTER CITY

'He went down like the Belgrano!'

Yet another Gaddafi call to prayer about a goalkeeping error came half-way through the Manchester City match at Roker.

And indeed, it had been a difficult day again. It started off with drinks in *The Speculation Inn* in Washington. *The Spec* was a known place for weird people. Marc had once bumped into someone who had a chopping axe embedded in his head. The injured man came in and ordered a pint and said to the landlord:

'Phone us an ambulance marra will yeah?' And sat down on his own to drink his pint as if it was a Saturday night out with their lass. No one in the pub but Marc seemed to be bothered about this behaviour; they carried on playing dominoes and talking. The ambulance arrived and the man left the pub with the paramedic, axe still intact, and gave a pleasant thank you to the landlord.

'Cheers marra, so long.'

He was never seen again.

Today the squad were in *The Spec* with other Washington lads. They often went there on match day before heading off for the ritual nine bottles of *Vaux Double Maximum* round in the snug at Mrs Lyle's *Howard Arms*. In the pub was a bloke who always drank up some of a person's beer if they foolishly went to the outside toilet. Marc told them to watch the bugger and be careful. Daft Billy was skint and his beer precious so he decided to be especially cautious and watched the man carefully while the lads were drinking and talking about last week's trip to Leicester.

'Champion night in Doncaster wasn't it,' Marc said to the gang.

'Aye, it was. Anyone heard from Charlie this week?' Billy asked.

'Nah. He might still be there, locked up still,' Marc grunted.

'No, he's back. I talked to him at work. He hasn't got his fur coat mind,' chuckled Billy.

His friends chuckled with the thought. They had pulled up into Doncaster after the match with three buses and two of the Doncaster Man Utd branch pulled up after. Hell on of course in town but what made them all laugh was that after closing time Charlie walked onto the bus wearing a full white mink coat, rapidly followed by half of Donny's finest men in blue who hauled him off the bus and banged him up. It appeared he had no idea how he'd acquired the fur coat.

'We got a great write up in the press mind,' Marc said, and pulled out another cutting he had in his wallet. This one wasn't the usual one about how big Sunderland's crowds were compared to Newcastle's during the Boxer Revolution but about the trip. It was from the Evening Chronicle and the mother of a Doncaster bride had written to the paper to say how their wedding reception was made more enjoyable and fun by the arrival of the bunch of Sunderland supporters on the drink who had hijacked her daughter's wedding but made it even more fun.

What had happened was that Billy had noticed a wedding reception in the annex of the pub they'd taken over. He had gone in to see if anyone would fall for his wooing charms and amazing good looks. He came back into the bar with the bride! Sometime later they were followed by her worried husband who had lost his true love to the Viking raiders. They both ended up drinking with the crazy lads in the bar. The families and friends were left wondering where they had gone and after some anxious times came in to join them. Everyone had a great time. Billy ended up around the back with a huge girl bridesmaid who threatened to beat him up if he didn't do it there and then. Bottling it big time, he pretended he needed a piss and did a runner back to the bus, yet again frustrated, but this time of his own volition.

He hadn't time to relieve himself so he peed into an empty *Brown Ale* bottle on the bus and he'd sparked out with the drink. He woke up about Scotch Corner and was dying for a drink and asked if anyone had a can or bottle of beer to drink. Manic Marc handed him the half full bottle of urine, Brown Ale flavoured, and he swallowed the lot and promptly fell asleep again. One week later in *The Spec,* Billy had no knowledge of his urine drinking memories, but Marc decided to cheer him up and tell him. And as Marc reminded him of Billy, always very *cockly* and prone to vomiting, promptly began cockling and ran outside and spewed up. Everyone laughed and drank up as they were late for *The Howard Arms.*

Billy came back, saw them all leaving and went to drink his pint up. It was empty. He realised the pint pincher had supped his beer and buggered off out of the other door. Running after his mates to the cars, he garbled out angrily to his mates what had happened. Marc told him that he was stupid as he'd warned him about the beer stealer before.

Billy said: 'Ah nah that man. I put me teeth in my beer glass before I went out to spew. That should stop anybody drinking a pint surely?'

Marc said, laughing: 'Well that it didn't stop that bugger.'

'No it bloody didn't,' Billy wailed and opening his mouth wide showing a huge gap he howled. 'The bastard stole me teeth as well.'

No one could stop laughing until they reached the town.

As they walked along Roker Avenue towards *The Howard* an extremely expensive and posh bus pulled up which carrying either the Manchester City team or their executives. The driver asked Marc where the ground was. He sent them back around the system, over the bridge and through Hendon and towards the A19 and the delights of the chemical wasteland that was Middlesbrough. Feeling really chuffed with himself at his kindness to his fellow man he proceeded to fleece his mates who were playing cards at *Chase the Ace* before they headed out to the match.

Happy with his winnings, Marc went to the bar. The barman looked him up and down and said: 'What shoe size are you mate?'

Marc looked at him wondering what the hell that had to do with ordering beer but as he was in good fettle he answered positively; 'I'm a size twelve.'

'Thought yeah might be near that,' the barman replied. 'I've got a pair that size upstairs I'll bring them down.'

Marc again looked at the strange man, shook his head, handed the money over, took his change and started to carry the bottles back and forwards. By the time he'd come to the bar for the last bottles the man had returned carrying a large pair of used trainers. 'Here mate will these fit you? Some daft bugger left them in here weeks ago. I kept them in case he came back for them. He hasn't so you can have them.'

Marc stared at the pair of dirty, worn trainers, probably infested with some fungal growth. He was unsure why these things happened to him. He normally blamed Ginger Gus for his misfortune but today he couldn't. He liked the landlord and the pub and really didn't want to tell him to stick them where he would normally tell someone. With unusual diplomacy he came up with a solution. 'Thanks a lot marra. But our lass has just bought me some the spit of them. Brand new ones; cost hor a packet. She'll get vexed if I start using them.'

The barman looked so disappointed that Marc nearly took them off him only to throw in the bin on the way to match but he just turned around and went back to fleecing his mates. It was always a bizarre place *The Howard.*

Trainerless, Marc headed with his friends out of the pub to the game, past the old Rope Works and Billy commented through his toothless mouth how all the lasses he met at the match and in Tiffs night club all smelled of the tar the lasses used to coat the ropes when working in this lovely environment. He always seemed to have a thing about tar for years afterwards: Coal tar perfume was always Daft Billy's fatal attraction to his ladies: an aromatic delight long gone folks may be pleased to know.

As they strolled along towards the match and the kick off the Man City executive bus crawled past them coming back from its detour to the joys of Teesside. It was stuck in the crowds with only minutes to go. The driver recognised Marc's tall body above the crowds and as the bus slowed down he opened the door and howled abuse at Marc for his jolly misdirection jape. Marc just stared at him smiling. Billy in his inimitable way jumped on the bus steps and he rammed his face into the bus driver's, his mouth open wide. He pointed to his boxer's squashed nose, spread flat across his face like a banana, and asked a very pointed rhetorical question through his toothless gums: 'How'd yeah like a fyess like this ya Manc bastard!'

The driver decided he didn't and closed the door on the maniac.

The day only got better at the match when Ginger Gus amused the boys with one of his own very personal japes. A bloke and his wife always stood in front of a crash barrier which was just to the right of the goal about a quarter of the way up from the pitch and in front of the lads who stood behind the barrier. Gus named him *Gino Ginelli* because he was a bit swarthy and looked Italian. He came from Marley Potts so maybe he was just a bit sun burnt with the baking sun there or he didn't like soap; no one knew, or cared. He was what you would call these days *a happy clapper* in that he seemed to enjoy the actual match, and not the drinking , moaning, and jolly japes that everyone else went for. He was always well-dressed and obviously was one of those men who spent the morning at Gateshead Metro Centre shopping with their lass rather than getting blooted in the local club. He cheered and clapped and generally talked lots of knowledgeable things about football. He was so happy and obsessed by football and the team that generally he was hated by all around.

Gus loved him as a target and continually took the piss out him and their lass. But he was so happy and content with his lot that he actually seemed to enjoy Gus's quaint banter about his new haircut, his lass's large bottom and her pouting lips.

'How man, hev yeah been injecting your gob with that bot tox that you've injected your bot with?' and: 'Did yeah hev yeah hair cut with a scythe?'

Yes, Gus loved them and they seemed to love him until the day Gus gave Gino a hernia and he pissed himself.

Gino wore smart jumpers and chinos when weather permitted – which was normally only the last match of the season. He had that chic habit, which all Marley Potts Italians must have, of tying the jumper around his body and letting it dangle behind him when it was warm. After listening to his endless happiness, excitement, clapping and constant commentary of the first half of the match, Ginger Gus decided to weld his Binns' acquired *Loro Piana* to the barrier. He loosened the arms and tied it tight in a double unbreakable knot. And then, one minute before half time a Sunderland master striker woke up and actually hit the bar. This cheered the happy clapping crowd up for a few seconds, especially Gino because he leapt up like a jack in the box on speed, clapping excitedly like a seal, as he always did. He threw himself forward in an effort to raise a Di Canio-like salute to his heroes and promptly doubled up, slipping on the stone terrace and ended upside down bent double, unable to move, suspended from the barrier by his jumper.

How the lads laughed!

His lass screamed: 'You bastards. Let him loose!'

Ginger Gus chuckled though his tash: 'He's enjoying hisel man,' and leant over the barrier and patted the Italian Stallion Mackem on his doubled-up back saying: 'How man, is thoo gonna give us arl another happy clap?'

The contorted man tried to straighten up and turn around but Gus had tied it so tight that he had little room to manoeuvre. His wife was struggling to loosen the knots and was pleading with the ginger jester and everyone to help.

Marc was staring straight ahead, anxiously waiting for the next half, totally uninterested in helping anyone, least of all anyone who was actually enjoying the match. He turned to his young son: 'When we get home tell yeah mother I'll not be in for tea, I'm going down to the Cardiff match on Tuesday night. We've got to win that one son.'

'I need a piss man. I'm bursting,' Gino Stallone, the Italian gallower cried out. 'It's halftime man. I always have a piss. The jumper's pressing on me bladder man.' And unable to turn, and in great stress he spoke to his wife in a way he'd never dared before: 'Get the bloody knots untied, you silly bitch.'

'Don't you talk to me like that!' His normally placid wife howled at him and she turned to the ginger tormentor: 'Let him loose you ginger bastard or I'll bloody deck yeah!'

'How man, divn't loose ya rag lass,' Gus slurred. And patting the hanging man again on his back: 'By your lass is tad feisty mate when she's vexed. Bet she likes it being tied up tee, eh? Kna what ah mean mate, eh?'

Bang! Gus gets hit around the head by her handbag bag full of *Marks and Spencers Metro Centre* prawn sandwiches.

'You ginger bastard. Let him loose or I'll get the poliss.'

'Alreet, calm down man,' Gus chuckled, dodging the swinging bait bag as he tried to untie his unbreakable knots.

'Hurry up man, please, for...oh!...shite...' and sadly a stain started appearing on his new light grey chinos. Gus loosed the last knot and the bloke ran like an Italian tank in reverse along and upwards to the heaving bogs. His wife followed after him raging back at the lads threatening to *get the poliss*. The two Italian lovers never appeared again. The poor man was probably consigned to a Saturday afternoon at *Fenwicks'* cafe like all the other strange tortured men who loved their wives more than the football.

Ginger Gus was sad they left and looked around for someone else to torment. He spotted the couple who always came to the game wearing two matching anoraks and a Tartan flask of cappuccino to share. *Porfect* he whispered to himself through his ginger tash. He staggered drunkenly towards them full of optimism.

And the rest of the actual match? Well, you can guess - Gaddafi said it all before: 'It sank like the Belgrano.'

CHAPTER THIRTEEN
Liverpool, Wrexham & Jilted Brides

End of season promotion or relegation cliff hangers are a nightmare for most clubs. The advent of the playoff system caused even more teams to fall into the relentless misery of an extended season. For Sunderland supporters for years and years it was almost every season that the team's safety or promotion and the supporters' happiness depended on the last game or couple of games and most times seemingly an away game on the final day of the season.

In early times it was games against Everton, Liverpool, Aston Villa, Wrexham, Wimbledon, Man City and then all the Wembley play off finals but in recent times there were some actually relatively happy results with the miracle rescue seasons of Di Canio, Poyet, Advocaat and Allardyce.

The seven or eight Wembley trips with nothing to come back with but gastric ulcers and hangovers were particularly hard to take. And always up and down the leagues like a *whoor's draws*. I could go on. However, those performances and records are for statisticians and this book is really meant for psychologists and criminologists, so I'd better move quickly on to real people. And that brings me to the vagaries of Scouse people and particular Liverpool trips.

'Be careful son; Watch where we are and get back safe,' John said to his fourteen year old nephew Stephen as he went off to buy a hot dog. They were standing crushed on the open terraces at Anfield. It was the last match of the season and as usual it was a nail biting end. It was between Norwich and Sunderland who went down from the First Division and Sunderland were playing the mighty Liverpool. Thousands had made the journey down and Sunderland had the whole of the end opposite the Kop. It was Stephen's first away match and as he had taken some time to come back, John was worried for him. He came from Shiney Row so wasn't too clued up about the real world. When he returned he was somewhat dishevelled and a bit bruised.

'What's happened son?' John asked, concerned.

'I got me hot dog and as I was walking past with my scarf all these lads with red scarves started shouting to me to come over to the fence. So I did to shake their hands. The bastards were Liverpool supporters weren't they. Never knew them bastards had the same colours as us, did I? They dragged me over the fence by my scarf and neck and started wedging into me. I managed to nut one and break free. Bastards got my scarf though.'

'I towld yeah,' Marc bent down and whispered in John's ear. 'Nivva bring anyone from Shiney to an away trip.'

Sadly, Stephen had a huge heart but his life experience at the time was limited to Shiney Row, which was the same as saying, he'd never left the Rift Valley. And Scousers, like most nutcases at football those days, would prey on anyone who showed lack of street awareness. But today was the day the pit village lads showed the Scousers who was smarter and tougher.

Ray Kennedy, born in the North East, who would end up an Arsenal, Liverpool and Sunderland stalwart, had a golden opportunity to score and level the game for Liverpool. John looked him in the eye as the ball fell to his feet, an open goal begged only six yards away. John swears to this day Kennedy looked at him in the crowd, smiled and sliced the ball way past the left hand post. He definitely lifted his head after and raised his hands in apology and smiled at the thousands who were cheering his miss. Liverpool missed so many chances that day and the tackles were so easy, and with the psychotic mad Jock, Souness, in the team, it was not too difficult to understand that having already won the league, Bob Paisley, a Sunderland supporter and pitman from Hetton-le-Hole, might well have had a quiet word with his team. Indeed, he sent a case of champagne to the players in the dressing room after.

The football always seemed good in Liverpool but the surrounding environment was always hairy. And the constant scams by the *scallies* had to be avoided and sometimes paid back.

Crazy Jim was a master at japes and was always up for fun with our Scouse friends. So it was that day. After the ecstasy of finally witnessing a last day rescue, the lads met up with Crazy Jim. He was in good form even though early on it looked like he had been scammed by a scally before the match into paying him money to watch over his car so that it didn't get wrecked. This was a normal occurrence in the Beatles' City. Kids asking for money or your car would be wrecked when you came back. He gave him money and said he'd double it if the car was ok after the game. When he got back with Paul, the lad, obviously greedy and a tad naive given the looks of Crazy Jim, was still there. They met the lad, laughed at his demand for his *protection money bonus* and promptly bundled him into the boot of the car. They thought that as he loved the car so much they would take him for a little ride – out of Liverpool, past Manchester and onto the road across the Pennines. They opened the boot some miles from Liverpool and left him there after relieving him of the fiver for the car parking.

Marc chuckled at this and told the assembled asylum of a story when he parked his BMW at Coxhoe Working Men's Club in Durham County. Some local pit lads' youths must have heard ·of the big city car protection scam and said: 'Your car's a cracker marra. It won't get harmed if you pay us a quid.'

Marc quickly thought he'd sort these daft hillbillies out: 'You'se better not gan near that car, me Rottweiler is in it - and he can open doors.'

One particular acne-faced youth came right up to him and looked up at the six foot four man and said: 'That's a clever dog marra. Can it put out fires?'

Marc paid the pound.

Years later Mick went to a Liverpool match against his beloved Newcastle. He took his wife for the weekend as they were Beatles fans and wanted to do the Liverpool Cavern scene. John arranged for him to go to the match with his two huge Geordie scaffolders who were working on the Liverpool Lime Street refurbishment and supported *the Toon.* They had invited their wives down for the match and a fun weekend in a city that was now rejuvenated and becoming a popular weekend away. They were all sat in a pub near Lime Street before the match. It was the scaffolder's local while they worked there. It still looked like something from *Boys from the Black Stuff,* with a wooden bar and fittings. Walnut lined walls and a lovely nicotine stained ceiling; an icon and memory of what it was like to die of emphysema through passive smoking with one Saturday night out in the bar. However, instead of *Shake Hands* and *Yossa* it had lots of shiny, worn out, blue pinstripe-suited, second-hand trainer wearing old men. Bizarrely, most wore trilby hats and were waltzing with flowery dressed or pinny wearing women. All were dancing to the cranky jukebox which was playing Matt Monroe, Nat King Cole, Gene Pitney and other crooners.

The Newcastle revellers were enjoying the nostalgic ambience of the bar without the normal *Toon* episodes of drunken lunatics asking if they were *looking at them* or *yeah calling my pint a puff?* Their ladies found themselves declining frequent invitations to dance with trilby and dodgy shiny-suited men when into the bar crashed a *Jack the Lad* type, He was bouncing on his feet with his slip on trainers, clearly on *E* or something else. He was years younger and totally out of place with the rest of the weird clientele. He promptly sat down at the same table as the three lads and their wives. He was twitching and jumping with drugs, nerves or just charva edge (more edge than a broken piss pot comes to mind) and trying to make conversation.

The two scaffolders grunted menacingly at the scally.

Mick as usual seeing the dark clouds appearing turns to his wife and whispered: 'Ah just kna this isn't gonna end well.'

The girls chatted briefly to him as he tried to break into the close knit group chatting about the football, the city and shops and things. Then one of them cries out: 'He's touching me leg!' and she moves her chair and looks down. She sees his bare foot move slowly back towards his chair and then realises that her handbag had been dragged under the boy's chair along with the other two girls' bags using only his bare foot while he calmly chatted to them. While he distracted them with his constant chatter, below the table, everyone was oblivious to his criminal podiatry. His discarded trainer was lying by his chair, which he'd obviously removed with his other foot so he could use his foot and toes to snaffle the handbags. Now his crime discovered, the lad leaps up, scoops up his trainer and hurtles quickly out of the door empty handed. By the time the two scaffolders had reacted he was long gone down into the crowds heading to the match.

'Thing was John, those lads of yours were massive, hard as nails and horrible looking bastards. Who the hell would risk deeing that to them?' a still shocked Mick told John when he returned back to civilisation.

'Scousers,' John replied.

A final story on parking monies in Liverpool that is legend is from the nineties when a few lads were parked up in some back street behind the Kop and being pestered by the usual blackmail money for their car's safety when a cute young lass comes up pushing a pram and asks for a pound for her baby. The lad telling the story found this surprising as she was about nine years old. Wisely, they decided to check on the authenticity of the 'virgin birth' and turning the covers over revealed a Jack Russell dog asleep with a can of Carlsberg Special Brew in its jaws; as the lad said: 'It's rough around there.'

WREXHAM

Two years before the Liverpool match that Bob Paisley and Ray Kennedy won for Sunderland, Marc, John and Billy headed to Wrexham for the final decider on automatic promotion. Still pissed from the night before, they put a crate of *Federation Special* onto the back seat of John's old Mini for the journey. The day didn't start well as they ran out of petrol at Chester. Marc was telling the story in a Wrexham pub to some lads and one of them said: 'You did alright then. Chester isn't far away from here.'

'We nivva got to Chester in Cheshire man, nivva got past Chester-le-Street. We set away from the Gardener's Club, Washington. This daft twat awnly got three miles,' explained Marc.

It didn't go much better when John decided to stop off at his fiancée's house off the M62 and wish her sister a happy wedding day.

'Weren't you invited?' Billy asked when John said they'd stop and say hello.

'Aye: But it was today wasn't it and I knew it was last match of the season so I told her mother I couldn't' mak it. Given how important it is now, pleased ah did'

Billy looked at the back of John's head from the back seat and said: 'Bah, if I'd have towld hor mother that she'd have gone mental.'

John chuckled and replied: 'She did. I'm banned from the house.'

'Lucky, lucky bastard,' Marc grunted.

When his mother-in-law visited, he spent most of the time standing in the garden in the rain leaning on a spade staring at his leek trench until she left hours later. As I said before he wasn't quite right in the head.

'But will she not gan daft at us torning up pissed man at her daughter's wedding if you're banned?' an astonished Billy asked.

'I'll just say hello to her sister and our lass and hope the mother is too worried about the wedding to bother chasing us. What the hell – gives us a chance to refill the beer supplies. These will be gone by Leeds.'

John's fiancé was delighted when he pulled up. Strangely, even after having the Roker Park pee soak her new shoes and the amorous attentions of the semi-erect charva, she loved him and his wayward ways those days. However, the mother was not amused when the bottles rolled out of the driver's seat open door and clattered towards her new wedding shoes. The horror for her was compounded by Daft Billy holding his groin and asked her in front of her posh friends: 'Can I use your piss nyueks missus? I'm borsting.'

Needless to say it was not a great homecoming and John decided a quick exit was sensible. A quick kiss to his distraught lass and one to her bemused sister and off he drove with the mother of the bride howling obscenities at the disappearing travellers.

'Close shave that,' Marc said, cracking open a can he'd just purchased at the slightly tinted, Yorkshire person's off licence where Billy had relieved himself against the side wall, to the shock of the natives. 'Gives me the horrors man; the sight of a man lead off to slaughter. Rather gan to me fatha's funeral than a wedding.'

And sure enough his wish came true. However, the funeral only started after a great day with many, many thousands of travelling supporters invading Wales. Two goals and a win for Sunderland,

and then, when everyone in the crowd who had personal radio's said that Stoke had drawn, which was the result Sunderland needed to go up to the first division, the three lads along with hundreds more climbed over the spiked fences to start another gardening episode of the Welshmen's pitch. Then the funeral chimes of doom rang out – in the form of the Racecourse ground's loud speakers which announced that Stoke had actually scored in injury time. This was of course in hindsight a poor decision by the Wrexham officials, as instead of gardening, the horticulturists turned into the Viking ancestors they had not evolved from and promptly launched an invasion of the Welsh end of supporters who were mocking the result. They didn't mock for long.

The long trip back was as gloomy as any funeral - or wedding.

MAN CITY

The lads were fated to get involved with weddings at matches, Billy stealing the bride at Doncaster, John being banned from his own sister-in-law's wedding at Wrexham and now at Manchester City, they were fated to help another poor lost soul. For yet again the lads were heading down the A1 all excited for another end of season final match, this time to save them from relegation. All roads to Manchester were packed with red and white cars, buses, vans - anything on wheels that could move. The lads headed down in John's car and John was looking forward to seeing some old haunts in Manchester again.

They parked up outside the White Lion in Fallowfield at 11.00 am. Years before it had sold excellent Robinson's beer and sure enough it still did. The lads were enjoying several beers when a man came in dressed in his top and tails wedding suit. He ordered a beer and large whiskey and sat near the lads. Ginger Gus was delighted as he saw an opportunity to take the piss.

'How man, is thoo ganning to a wedding when the lads are playing a git important game like today man,' he rhetorically asked, hoping for some bite to strike into.

'Yes, I'm supposed to be going to mine,' the man said dolefully looking at a picture of what the lads could only assume was his intended bride. 'I've decided not to go.'

If he was hoping for any sympathy, he was in the wrong company. Ginger Gus perked up. *Champion* he thought *this'll be a good un.*

'Your lass been shagging your best mate?' he stammered. 'The clip of hor in that picture, ah wouldn't blame yeah if yeah dumped hor."

The lad seemed not to understand Durham pitmatic or didn't care and he just carried on. 'No I love her. It's not for me I think - marriage. I can't go ahead. The wedding is at one and I've had a few already since breakfast. I'm not going to turn up.'

'For ****'s sake let's get out of here,' Marc said to John. 'This miserable bastard is an unlucky omen. My guts are ganning mental with worry, the biggest match in years and this twat whinges on about his wedding. I'm tempted to knock the **** out. That'll stop the unlucky twat whinging on.'

John told Marc to shut up and take another Gavsicon. With a lot more sympathy and empathy than his two mates he then asked the man what was problem. The man proceeded to tell them a tale of his woes and doubts about being a good husband. After three sentences Marc, held his head in his hands, got up and went to the bar to cool off.

After the depressed man showed them more pictures of his fiancée, Ginger Gus tried to get another bite:

'By ****, she's got an ugly fyess. Bit of a fat lass tee. Mebbies some tar brush in hor? Nee wonder you are not ganning to the wedding.'

Still he wouldn't bite and after asking him, if their lass farted in bed - 'Bet it smells like a styehble eh?' - and getting no response Gus gave up .

Billy and Keith started playing dominoes. Marc had heard enough and he came back with three large whiskeys and plonked them down in front of the morose bridegroom and said: 'Here you miserable twat get these down yeah. Yeah divn't knaar how lucky yeah are to escape yor lass and hor mother man. Let me tell yeah about how many times we've beaten the Mags and when this ginger twat fell under a bus. Now, that'll cheer you up.'

Several whiskeys later the bridegroom was draped in a Sunderland scarf and singing: '*Aye, Aye, Ippee. If you hate Newcassel clap your hands!*'

Marc was delighted this might be a lucky omen and Ginger Gus was delighted as he had managed to empty the bridegroom's wallet of four rounds of beer and whisky.

'How long to get to the church mate?' John asked.

'It's just around the corner. My best man will be waiting for me there and wondering what's happened. What do you think I should do?'

'Top your ******* sel,' Marc shouted over. 'It'll be what you'll want to do every day after you marry, you daft twat.'

'Get another round in mate. It'll help yeah forget that ugly fyess your lass has. Here, I'll tak that last fiver in your wallet and get them in for yeah.'

Ginger Gus took the lad's wallet and went off for yet another round.

John tried to end the pain and counselled the confused groom: 'If I were you mate I'd go to your wedding. Everyone gets nervous. Look at Marc there man. He's a nervous wreck about the match every day of his miserable life. And he was just as nervous when he got married. I was his best man and to get him to walk to the altar we had to drink the bottle of communion wine up in the vestry in the Carlisle church when the vicar put us in there to sign things before the wedding. Chucked us out pissed into the church. Their lass's mother has nivva smiled since.'

'Sod it,' the man said suddenly, staggering up mortal drunk, he slurred out: 'You...lads...have helped...so, so...so much. I'm' h...h...heading...to my wedding....,' and he moved to the door. Ginger Gus went over and took his hand out of his pocket as he approached the wobbling man. The bridegroom in his joy thought his new found mate was coming to shake his hand and wish him well and with a look of great joy he put out his hand.

Gus looked puzzled at the outstretched hand and turned it over and placed the man's last ten pence coin in his palm and said: 'Here son, you tak this for the collection box. It'll mak you feel better. Ah always thowt giving is much better than receiving.'

And he pushed him out of the door.

The wedding counsellors moved on to visit some pubs in Moss side which John could remember going to in the Seventies. They had changed somewhat and not so welcoming now he wasn't a naive and non-threatening young student, so, after a few encounters with the natives, they followed the screaming sirens towards the ground. The pubs were full of crazy Man City or even crazier Sunderland fans and they couldn't squeeze in. They were well pissed anyway so they piled into an off-licence and John bought a two litre bottle of hooch cider. As they approached the ground John gave the bottle to Gus to take in through the turnstile into the half of the Man City Kippax End that many of Sunderland had been given. Two police took objection to them taking strong drink into the ground and ordered them to leave it there on the floor next to the turnstile.

'Bugger that,' Gus said and starts to sup it. He swallows about a pint and gives it to John who sits down to try to finish the rest.

The policeman stands next to Ginger Gus as John gives him the bottle back and says: 'I've never seen so much drink at a match. Have you daft bastards up there not got smaller bottles?'

'This is a small bottle man where we come from,' the ginger man quipped as he supped the last quarter and staggered into the ground.

The unofficial figure had 15,000 Sunderland supporters inside Maine Road that Saturday in May 1991 hoping to see them win and avoid relegation yet again. It was an amazingly emotional game. It started with a mini war between the fans separated on the Kippax Stand by a double line of police which carried on throughout the game. It ended with them all shaking hands, swopping shirts and scarves through the amazed and stunned police line. Sunderland were beaten and relegated by a player soon to be their hero in another life, Niall Quinn. However, that day the noise, the emotion and the support of the Sunderland fans had numbed both police and Man City fans. Denis Smith, the manager, in tears at what he witnessed, kept bringing out the players to thank the fans. Many of the supporters were in fancy dress; Arabs, Snow White and the Seven Dwarves, Robin Hood, you name it -

and all singing, Monty Python's iconic, *Always Look On The Bright Side Of Life*.

John turned to Keith as they stood with the hordes on the Kippax and said: 'Dear God, Keith, and this is when we were relegated. What would it be like if we actually won something?'

He turned around and took one last look at the crowd and the pitch and picked Gus up. He shook him conscious.

Gus yawned: 'Did I miss owt?'

'Nah Gus, time to gan yaem mate.'

'Any cider left?' Gus asked as he turned to leave with his mate.

'Plenty in the car son - plenty,' John muttered compassionately.

'Champion,' said a thirsty Gus, 'I hope yeah are driving.'

It was a long drive back home again.

CHAPTER FOURTEEN
Carlisle, Sir John Hall & Corporate Hospitality

Long journeys home either ecstatic or manically depressed sat in cars, mini buses, transit vans or coaches are what following your team all is about, the monotony of the journey only broken by the bizarre behaviours of your colleagues and meetings with rivals in similar mental states. Manic Marc was always focussed on one thing either the match ahead or the next match so he really was never up for any enjoyment or fun after any match - win or lose. Wembley trips sadly exaggerated these psychological traits.

The FA cup final with Liverpool was no exception to his angst. Marc had used his brand new school minibus as the travelling septic tank. He was Head of a school and in days when he was not worrying about 'the lads' he actually lead a great school (yep folks, those great days, even those people who may have what the sociologists these days call *issues*, could be Heads of schools. I know one, a loyal Sunderland supporter, who has been knighted for God's sake. I never knew boxing was a quality recognised by Her Majesty's Department of Education? But heh, if it helps control the little cherubs in the school who am I to complain. The new minibus was only going to be used for one thing – taking Marc and his long suffering mates to Wembley.

After a long drunken journey down the M1 the bus pulled up in a leafy suburban street of Watford where the walk to the pubs and Underground wasn't far. There was a bloke with a clipboard writing down the registration numbers of the parked cars. The squad and driver ignored him and walked off hurriedly to get to the pubs. Marc stopped and watched him, getting agitated and vexed. He decided to ask what he was up to: 'What are yeah deeing mate?'

'I'm a resident here and as you don't have a permit these cars will be privately clamped.'

Marc asked: 'Dee yeah live here like?'

The extremely naive neighbourhood watch and community carer said: 'Of course that's my house there.' He pointed to a lovely detached property.

Marc looked backwards and forwards for witnesses and seeing none he looked down at the now worried man, wrapped his big hand around his neck and explained the laws of away trips. 'Champion, now I know which windows to hoy the bricks through if I come back and you've clamped us.'

After losing the FA cup final and the miserable return on the tube and a few beers in the pub, Marc was pleased the only vehicle from up North in that posh street that wasn't clamped was his mini bus; definitive proof that the UK's education system was much better in those days when violence and intimidation by Headmasters was still allowed.

Manic Marc's propensity for distress before, during or after a match could erupt into more physical educational instruction for students who had not read the manual on Educational Psychology. Cue one agitator from a small County town ending up lying in the toilets in a pile of urine very much asleep. He had not expected a very obsessed and cerebrally driven Headmaster to drive twenty miles to get a signal on the radio for a Sunderland match sitting alone in his car in the dark satanic hills, popping a box of Gaviscon tablets down his throat and then driving down to town and into the pub for a welcome pint at halftime. This particular student should not have followed a well-dressed, senior tormented man into the toilet and threatened him and commented adversely on this new arrival's football team and his paternity.

And another Physical Education lesson...

'George, sorry I'll have to leave mate. If anyone asks, I was nivva in your box – don't want to get you in trouble, reet?'

As relayed by a well-dressed professional to George, a business man who could book hospitality at many grounds. Manic Marc had been enjoying his mate George's corporate box hospitality at one ground in a quite important and sectarian match. He left for the Executive toilets and it seems another man had confronted him in the corporate toilets yet again with comments about the faecal matter that was his team and how he thought the kind, caring, but wound up man, might be lacking a father. Another lesson plan completed.

The local news on Monday had lots of bulletins decrying the problems of trouble after the match, and 'even in the corporate area' – I don't think it had any co-incidence mind to teaching practice.

And yet another seminar...

'I was with you Wednesday mate if the poliss call?" and the phone went down.

Must be just another co-incidence George thought, when he got Marc's telephone call after watching the TV news of a slight altercation with two people over local football geography in a city centre bar at 11.30 am on a normal weekday morning.

And a yet another safe guarding symposium...

'What the hell is that bump on yeah heed man?' George asked Marc as he sat in the corporate box enjoying a brilliant cup victory for once. The bump had begun as a slight bruise but it grew as the second half went on into something resembling Kilimanjaro

'Bit of bother with couple of supporters who happened to fall down the stairs into the main reception after they noticed me Sunderland tie and started to get micey and angry about where I was born. It seems they tripped on a bag of '*Walkers*' crisps. I must have bumped me forehead trying to help them.'

He borrowed a hand mirror from the ladies who were serving food and drink and checked the huge protrusion on the side of his bald head: 'Ah must be getting out of teaching practice.'

When he was at the peak of his practice, as a solid citizen and respected educationalist in the area, his joy knew no bounds when he and his family were invited by Bob Murray, the Sunderland Chairman at the time, into the Directors seats for a Southend match. His long suffering wife was really looking forward to being treated to nice food and drinks and actually spending a match day with her husband. Everything was going splendidly, as the posh writers might write, until the opposition scored and the crowd got extremely restless. These were days of the endless misery of Terry Butcher as manager and the crowd had reached boiling point. Someone from the seats in the Main Stand adjacent to the Directors box threw abuse at the Directors and to those sat with them, followed by screams and abuse from a lot more supporters.

When a cup of hot Bovril was thrown at our educationalist and one man leaned over and spat at his family, no doubt never thinking the Director's box would contain a raving psychopath, Marc felt he had to intervene and try his undoubted diplomacy skills homed during other corporate box disputes of the type I have recently mentioned. Sadly these mediation skills didn't impress either the unconscious Bovril drinker or the police and he and family were escorted out surrounded by police dogs, Alsatians snapping at his wife's new Bali shoes and ripping her Laura Ashley dress, and a howling mob spitting and throwing missiles at her. It seemed to spoil the ambience of her first day out at a match.

As the years rolled on George took a box many times at Sunderland at the brand new Stadium of Light. Marc came in useful at one night match when the box bar had run out of beer after the match. He had as a young man at school learnt many things, none of them to do with school work as you would think for a professional Head Teacher, but lots about how to pick the locks of the tuck cupboard or the social club money box, stack a deck of Three Card Brag and fix a dog race. These were life skills that came into use that night.

George had hired Lee Clark's empty box and next door was Peter Reid's own empty box. Dinky Derek had climbed over into the scouse man of 'Simian looks heed' box from the lads' one and tried in his inimitable way to smash into the drinks cupboard. It needed the lock-picking skills of Marc using a bent tea spoon, not the scaffold pole thumping skills of Dinky, to prise the precious bottles of booze out and into the extremely drunk hands of the only people left in the stadium. They stripped it bare of all drink. Sorry Peter to tell you this, but I'm sure you could have afforded it.

Suddenly, the floodlights came on again and the men looked out from the box over the stadium and field and young Keith, shocked yet again at all the antics, pointed and exclaimed: 'Dear God it's that mate of yours John. He's half naked, howling at the lights!'

And sure enough it was. Derek had decided to strip off and have a dance on the pitch with a bottle of Vodka in his hand and sing the anthem that had seen him battered many times in Newcastle and Tyneside bars – 'Red Army! Red Army!'

The security guards woke up and escorted the half-naked singer back to Lee Clark's asylum and eventually to his home.

Marc met Lee Clark not long after that at another corporate hospitality event. He'd been invited to a Newcastle Falcon's Rugby night match and as it was work he had to go. As he didn't give one fig for Rugby or anything to do with Newcastle, he wore his Sunderland AFC tie and decided instead of going to watch the Rugby match in his posh seat after the corporate table dinner he would go into the bar and watch the England football match from Wembley that was on TV that night. He stood at the bar and ordered a drink. A man came up beside him and the staff rushed over to serve him. Marc turned to see who it was who was so well looked after and it was Sir John Hall, the Chairman of Newcastle, the man who had founded the Falcons and moved Newcastle United into challenging for the Premiership and Champions League. Of course he was the devil incarnate to Marc but Sir John spotted Marc's tie and entered into conversation:

'I see you're a Sunderland supporter. Are you not watching the rugby tonight?'

'Nah. I only came for the beer and work. I'm corporate. I can't stand England football but it's better than rugby. I only ever watch Sunderland.'

'I'm like you. I came in to watch the first half. Prefer football to rugby.'

'If you like football why'd you buy those black and white buggers then?'

Sir John laughed: 'I fell for that didn't I. Let me get you a drink.'

As he bought the drink, Lee Clark entered with three Newcastle United players and they looked surprised to see their Chairman and nodded respectfully at him. Lee Clark came over to buy some drinks and he too spotted Marc's tie. In fact he couldn't help looking at it. Marc thought, *Got yeah you bugger.*

Lee Clark was a very good footballer in Peter Reid's amazing team but he was always tainted as he was a true Newcastle United graduate and supporter. Despite his professional and skilled performances for Sunderland there were many (Marc included) who believed his loyalties always lay with Newcastle. This was proven in many people's eyes when his career at Sunderland ended prematurely when he was caught in the *tee-shirtgate* scandal. He was photographed on the way to another Newcastle Wembley defeat wearing a tee-shirt with *Sad Mackem Bastards* on it. He would never play for Sunderland again. This was to be a couple of months in the future, which was possibly just as well given big Marc's angst anyway about him playing for his beloved lads.

Sir John bought another drink for the pair and said that he'd have to go at half time to be seen at the rugby and he asked jokingly if Marc had enjoyed chatting with a Newcastle Chairman.

'Ah wouldn't have given you the shite off my shoe but ah kna in my heart yeah are Sunderland supporter. Everyone knaar's you had a season ticket with us.'

'That's right I did. A lot of us in Northumberland watched both teams. Sunderland was my favourite at the time.'

'Then why the hell did you buy those buggers?'

'Money, mate,' Sir John answered truthfully. 'At the time Newcastle United was a hell of an opportunity and price. They were and are the best brand and along with the Metro centre and all my other plans for Newcastle, rugby, the Arena it all fitted together.' He smiled and said rhetorically: We've done ok haven't we?'

'Have yeah shite! Yeah've won nowt, and as for yeah crowds - look here ah'll show yeah...,' and Marc began to extract his wallet and pull out his faded newspaper cutting of past crowd attendances.

Laughing, Mr Hall placed his hand on Marc's wallet. 'That's all right Marc. It was great to meet you. Best of luck with Sunderland. I really hope you win promotion.' And he shook the demented Marc's hand and left.

Yes, nothing much has changed over the years with the big man. Cancer, age, no widower's pension yet or a good football team to dull his worry or his passion. Indeed, not long ago even in his Educational retirement he was engaged in some reminisces of his old day's escapades.

'You old English twat. I'm gonna have yeah!' The young large man in the Kilmarnock shirt climbed out of his car as he shouted his racial hatred. Unfortunately, the young man in the nice new Range Rover car who had had a bumper bump with Marc in a car park, didn't expect a six foot four retired teacher to lumber out of his old rusty car, take his very sharp chopping axe from the driver's side pocket where he had kept it fondly for years for opportunities like this, and chase the terrified youngster past the pharmacy. He then stopped, a bit out of breath these days, old football knees knackered and giving up and went in to pick up his medicines. His son sat in the passenger seat reading last week's football programme and shook his head at yet again another day of character building parental guidance.

Yes, Marc was passionate in his misery.

CARLISLE

John was similar in his levels of passion but not for football or local rivalry. Rather his desire to have a few beers without anyone upsetting him. Trips away were lifelines from a life of business and pressure and managing seriously deranged people, whom he had much in common. Always things seemed to go astray with his search for karma and nirvana

Trips to the North West were always good fun because the lads ended up back near Carlisle and a pub called *The George,* which had as many very strange people in it as George Lucas had intended in Star Wars. After a particularly difficult day at Preston, after the match John and Marc and their two kids were faced with five arseholes outside the ground. After a short interlude, which didn't end well for those who thought family men were fair game, they took a shorter trip up the usual wet the M6 with one windscreen washer working and the knackered alternator only powering very dim headlights and a very drunken driver trying to see through the mist. They pulled into *The George.* If you have watched *An American Werewolf in London,* well, you'll know what I mean about the ambience.

It started with Marc chatting to his friend Brian from the village; a small stocky very hard man with a propensity for drinking long and hard and with a brother who had certain marital problems. 'How's your brother's divorce ganning Brian?' Marc asked.

'Shite Marc. Those lawyers really wind you up, eh.'

'Thowt it was his lass that wound him up marra?'

'Well, she has got worse. Wants this, wants that. He thought he had a deal then the lawyer and her come up with another split. So last night he got pissed and wound up again so he took his chain saw and kicked the door down and sawed up everything half and half; the stair case, beds, tables and telly and the lot. He's just got out of the slammer. Let's see what the lawyers make of that, eh. See you had a shite result today. Carlisle didn't do well either, eh.'

'Aye, it was a shite match.'

And Marc who'd forgotten the match immediately after the whistle bought his good mate a drink to make up for his brother's extended stay at Her Majesty's pleasure for his version of the judgement of Solomon. He looked over at the pool area where it was all going well and where John was playing pool. Then a *Burberry* wearing type he'd beaten and who had wound them all up all night with his football hatred said: 'You know I canna stand you Mackems, eh. I can ring the Border City lads and they'll be here in minutes and we'll **** you mate.'

John took his cue in two hands and rammed it up into the man's throat and lifted him four inches off his feet against the wall. He asked him a very pertinent question. 'And how are yeah gonna phone them before yeah choke?'"

Needless to say, he never got to the phone, not because of John but because the boys in that pub were as sound as you will ever meet. Sultzy, was one of the characters that John Sullivan with *Fools and Horses* or Alan Bleasdale and *Boys From The Blackstuff* would have made famous. He came over when he saw John's little fracas and advised the edgy man to leave.

'John, he's not part of those mad BCF bastards. I had bother with him and three of his mates who jumped me when I was mortal in Brampton. They knocked me down and gave me a kick or two and I got up and scattered them. I looked at that twat lying on the groond and his mates standing yards off and told them: *I've had rougher sex* and I walked back into the pub eh.'

Marc was standing at the bar not too bothered with the bit of fuss. A man who had been standing there at the bar not saying much but observing came over and said to Marc: 'Heh marra, you must have been to Preston today? I was there with the lads over there. I'm a Sunderland lad. We're stopping over here at a bed and breakfast.' And having noticed the small altercation in the pool area he looked worried. 'It's a bit rough in here mate? We're not looking for trouble. Have you been here before?'

'Aye a few times,' Marc said. 'This is a canny pub mate, no problems with locals normally, unless you get micey twats in like that one chowking ower there. Just enjoy yersel. There's a quiz or summit on here soon.'

'I used to like a quiz and I ran one in Sunderland a few years ago before the match,' the stranger said.

'Dee yeah not dee it now?' Manic Marc asked, supping his beer.

'Nah never! Ever since a big maniac jumped on stage and accused us of cheating and grabbed me by the throat and lifted me up against the wall. It was all because my mate's table won the game and beating him by one answer. I always remember those mental scary eyes before I blacked out and hearing him screaming that no one except him would know the atomic number of Plutonium. The crazy bastard thought the game was fixed. Then one of his mates, some monster looking Hairy Hells Angel in a balaclava threatened the table's quiz captain with a gun. A gun for ****'s sake. All over a science quiz question. His nutcase nephew thumped the Domino card lad as well for announcing somebody had won. Mind you he might have had a point, Sammy the Chin was running it and the winner hadn't even been in the pub. But there was nee need for that. Mental cases that lot. Gave up after that, wasn't worth the risk. I've just had a flashback with that incident in the pool room over there. Fair knocked me back that. The doctor advised I run bingo in an Aged Miner's Club now before the match. It's safer.'

Marc remembered it all well but felt best not tell that to this still traumatised bloke. He looked over the man's shoulder and at his slightly deranged mate sitting on the pool table chatting and laughing with Sultzy and thought *He never did get over losing that quantum physics question to a table of dole wallas.*

He counselled the stranger in his new career choice from quiz host to bingo caller as only Manic Marc could: 'Aye mate, some people tak things like that seriously. Supporting the lads in any way or form is character building.'

Marc and the boys had tried the poor man's quizzes in the pub but as few of them ever watched normal TV except John Wayne or Clint movies, they were always stumped on TV programmes or sport other than Sunderland AFC. TV soaps or music were particularly problematic, so they used to send the kids down to the shop to buy the Radio Times and ITV magazines for the answers to the clues. Marc used to pop into the bar and phone *The George* up on the pay phone and talk to his great Everton mate Don, a polymath in sport knowledge. Yes, it was still possible to cheat before the advent of smart phones. But curiously, despite the collective university honours degrees, post graduate qualifications and outright cheating, none of them could ever beat the team that sat with the actual Quiz Master. This consisted of a small group of dole walla's, shot blasters and ex welders who appeared to know more than the man on *The Chase* ever would about Quantum Mechanics and the writings of Descartes. It must have been some school that they had had attended in Southwick!

Mackie came over to talk to Marc. One look at the starey eyes and scars and the Quiz Master drank up quickly and did a runner to his mates. At that moment he'd realised that he'd stumbled into Cumbria's own *Slaughtered Lamb Pub* bar and he'd best sup up and get to the bed and breakfast safely, long before the howling at the moon started. Those of you, like my son, who have never watched *American Werewolf in London* and seen the pentangle, silver bullets and the clip of the folks in *The Slaughtered Lamb* watch it - you'll understand.

It was indeed a wise decision. Although he could be extremely nice and friendly, Mackie, like the American werewolf, had a teensy, weensy temper which manifested itself in extreme violence. Now as he stood next to his friend, he was banned again for the season from local and national football because of his passion for playing the game. Very few pubs and clubs allowed him in their premises due to his physical debates with security and anyone who fancied their chances against him. He rarely lost these debates. He was good at his hobby – violent mayhem. He also supported Man Utd.

'Good match last week Marc?' Mackie asked his tall, manically depressed mate about the pub team football team game.

'Aye. I hear we were lucky to draw. If you'd have been playing you daft twat they might have won.'

'Sorry about that,' the tortured Irishman said, 'You know what it is mate. I'll sign up next year when the ban is over, eh.'

Marc did indeed *know what it is*. Sadly, so did the centre half and two innocent onlookers who ended up in casualty.

'Pity about Brodie, if he was playing it might have made a difference eh,' Mackie said.

'Guess it would if the daft bugger hadn't broken his legs. What happened ? I heard a riding accident,' Marc replied.

'Hah Hah...it wasn't so much a riding accident as a diving one. We were coming back from an August match one day after a few on the train and spotted a horse, well a pony, in the field next to the river. Brodie says he can ride hosses eh. So we bet him a round of drinks and he lowpes on the back of this pony and rides it around the field like a Red Indian, grabbing its mane. The hoss is trying to throw him off eh.'

'Dear God, he's mental. Was he thrown off and knackered his legs?'

'No Marc. The daft bugger rode the hoss until he lowped off. He then says he's boiling hot as the weather was scorching - had been for weeks. So he climbs on Wetheral Bridge and decides to go for a swim to cool off. The bugger jumps and breaks both his legs – the watta was only a foot deep because of the drought eh.'

'Aye that'll dee it,' Marc said, uninterested in the outcome or Brody's recovery.

Moving off the touchy subject of FA Disciplinary Tribunals and the mad rodeo high diver he asked the demonic football genius, 'Did you enjoy your match and trip to Paris then?'

'Aye we did Marc. United weren't very good but the trip was great. I didn't get locked up and neither did Sultzy, so that was a bonus.'

'I heard the daft bastard forgot where his hotel was?' Marc asked.

'Aye, daft bugger eh. We all buggered off to meet some United lads and he said he'd go and get pissed and see what was around. After a few drinks he tried to find his way back but was lost and had nee idea where his hotel was or what it was called. So he jumped a cab and managed to get the Frog to understand him and drive around looking. They go around and around for about half an hour. Sultzy notices the cab is now fifty Euros so he says **** this, asks the driver to stop as this is his hotel and then does a runner down the back street. As you do.'

'Aye, I'm sure it's wise to dee a runner from a cab in Paris with them mad gun-toting police,' Marc replied.

Mackie continued; sarcasm lost on him: 'Anyway, he finds another bar and gets more drunk.'

Marc chuckled: 'That's no surprise.'

'No, I guess that's Sultzy. But then he remembers he had visited a whoor house before he went on the piss and given the lass his hotel card for later. So the daft bastard thinks he'll go get the card back and find the address. So he does no more than he jumps another cab to the whoor house. The bouncer in charge tells him to wait but he runs in and asks for the lass. He's told she's with a client a room behind the madam. The daft bastard runs through to the room and opens the door and lifts the client off his lady friend by his neck and asks the lass for his card back and where his hotel was. The daft bugger never made the match either eh.' He supped a long drink and said: 'Daft bugger has been done three times now for the drink driving. Police and court sent him for medical reports eh ' He shouted over to Sultzy at the pool table: 'Heh, Sultzy, how'd yeah get on with the Doc's this week?'

Sultzy looks back over and said: 'All my tests were ok. The doctor was amazed when he knew how much I drank. I was surprised me self and said to the doctor.' '*What have you got to dee doctor to do damage to yeah body? I must be deeing something wrang eh*' He threw me out, the bugger.'

All at the bar shook their heads they'd heard it all before.

A young couple came in and asked if there was any food on the menu. Bobby, Cumbria's most laid back landlord shook his head and grunted: 'Nowt left. All been scoffed.'

'Oh that's a pity. We just wanted a snack. Have you no sandwiches left?' the strangers asked.

Bobby was about to tell them to bugger off when he had an idea. 'I've got egg mayonnaise if you want them?'

'Great. Can we have two? My wife likes the mayonnaise made with Dijon mustard and Extra Virgin Oil please?'

Bobby looked at the man blankly for a few seconds. Marc turned to Brian and Mackie and whispered: 'For ****'s sake the only extra virgin Bobby has ever seen was when he was in Brampton juniors. This should be fun.'

Bobby just shook his head at the two customers and said: 'Aye, if that's what she wants eh,' and poured them their drinks and walked towards the end of the bar.

The two customers found two stools sitting next to three *Care in the Community* escapees. They looked rather disappointed in the whole ambience. They moved the woolly jumpers and walking sticks off the table and managed to get enough space for their two drinks and for two plates of their much anticipated sandwiches.

Meanwhile, Bobby had opened the large pickled egg jar on the bar which was half full and had been sat there since his pub football team celebrated winning the league ten months ago. He put his big unwashed hand into the jar and pulled out one and then another egg and handed the eggs to his daughter.

'Here tek these and there's a loaf of *Co-op* sliced breed and some *Heinz Salad Cream* in the kitchen. That should dee lass eh.'

And indeed it did. When Bobby's daughter brought the sliced bread and pickled egg with Heinz salad cream sandwiches in her hands and then handed them individually to them without plates, the customers were stunned. They thought about complaining but by now they too had fallen into the matrix of surrealistic charm which was *The George*. Bobby was talking to a crowd of clearly disturbed customers, and the daughter, avoiding any conflict or guilt, had hurried through the cast of *Scary Movie* into the safety of the kitchen. So, after squeezing each other's hand in comfort they ate them silently, without complaining. They rubbed the vinegar and salad cream off their hands onto their trousers and quickly supped up.

They left the pub without anyone noticing or caring and as they opened their car door, they heard a distant howl. The young lady looked up at the clouds in the dark sky. Ominously they parted, revealing a white harvest moon which bathed them and the car park in silver shadowy moonlight. Another howl and the couple leapt into the car, the man shaking and struggling to get the keys out of his pocket. Eventually, after what seemed an eternity he found the keys. Shaking uncontrollably he forced them into the lock and turned the engine. 'Thud!' something, hit the back of the car. Terrified, the lady was frozen with fear and unable to look around. Her partner tentatively glanced in the mirror; petrified he might see the sum of all his fears of this disturbing evening. He saw an unkempt, lupine form sprawled over his rear window. Its front limb was clutching and clawing at the top of the car. Horrified, with his hand shaking, the driver put the car in gear and put his foot down and the car leapt forward. As he turned the wheel to screech onto the A69 and safety, he looked out of his side window behind him. The animal which had been clutching at his car had toppled over onto the dirt of the car park. Accelerating past the pub they both looked over at the horrible creature which was now on four legs crawling towards the packed pub.

Then, another body appeared through the light from the pub doorway. It was Bobby heading to the Co-op to buy another bottle of Chateau George for another sad, deluded visitor to his asylum. He stopped dead in his tracks on hearing the inhuman sound emanating from the four-limbed creature's mouth as its chest was rising up and down in an attempt to remove some human detritus plainly stuck in its hideous throat. He moved hesitantly out of the pub and he stood still at the sight. His head moved backwards and his hands went up in front of him as he recognised the beast for what it was and what it had done.

'For God's sake, Titch, if you are going to puke on a customer's car, leave the mess on their car and not my car park. You drunken bastard! Get up on your feet and get back in the bar. You're next on the pool table eh.'

The next time the couple were in Cumbria they went to *Talkin Tarn* for lunch.

Brian and Marc oblivious to the horrors of outside had watched the whole sandwich episode and smirked through it all. Brian said to Marc: 'Remember when Bobby got the phone call to book the pub for a bus full of people heading from Birmingham to Scotland for a Wedding? They said they wanted a buffet and drinks. Bobby made twenty fower bacon sandwiches in sliced breed. He bought ten bottles of cheap Co-op wine from next door. When they arrived, remember his face?'

Marc laughed. 'Aye I dee. It was funny as owt. Twenty four Asians come walking in. All women's heed's covered in burkhas and men with white dresses and hats on. Bobby's fyess man! You couldn't mak it up!'

'Aye all Muslims eh,' Brian said smiling. 'Bobby warmed up and sold all the bacon sandwiches to the Sunday pub footie team the next week for ten bob each the tight bastard.'

Marc laughed and remembered another Bobby and food story. 'Remember when that couple came in for lunch and the bloke said they like fine wine and did Bobby have any. Bobby looked shocked, he nivva had any wine. But he nivva lost a customer so he said aye he had loads. He'd just open a bottle of the best for a tenner and they could have that. The two were ower the moon eh. Bobby just went next door and went to the Co-op and bought the Co-op special for thirty bob. He never put the bottle on the table but when they shouted for more he filled up the glasses over at the bar.'

Brian smiled. 'Yeah, he is some landlord. Best one was when he booked owld Tom's grandson's twenty-first eh. He filled the bar end with twenty of the maddest young un's in the area. They were jumping ower tables and the music blasting out. Lasses with skirts up to their arse. Lads groping them on the seats in the empty open lounge end. Bobby had put food and sandwiches in another area for another party and they thowt they were theirs too. Great party ganning on eh.'

Marc chuckled. 'Aye, a hell of a party and then into the pub troops the old folks from Brampton and their relations in tears, all dressed in black.'

Brain interjected. 'Aye Bobby had booked the other half of the open pub for a funeral. Nay separation between anyone; there was hell on. Two pay days at once for the tight bugger eh.'

Marc stood and looked over to Bobby, John, Sultzy, Brian, his brother, Don, Ginger Gus, Daft Billy , Olwd Keith and the residents of the local asylum and then back to his crazed friend Mackie. They all seemed to take this type of behaviour as normal. He smiled, despite the afternoon's terrible game and as a result felt content for once. And then he remembered there was a game next week. He panicked, heart racing slightly. He reached for his tablets, and feeling there was still at least one strip left, he calmed. He took the fixture list out of his wallet and planning in his tormented brain the trip to the match after the next one. He drank his beer and ordered the next round

CHAPTER FIFTEEN
Derby Day Again, Oldham & Asthma

'Call me an ambulance!' Ginger Gus shouted out after falling mortal drunk under a bus on Roker Avenue.

'You're an ambulance,' John said, bursting into laughter.

'Leave the Ginger bastard. We've no time for him. It's nearly kick off,' Manic Marc growled and hurried off, his long lanky legs and determination taking him straight through, and scattering, a bunch of elderly couples enjoying a stroll to the sea.

'I might have broken me leg man,' Ginger Gus howled as the concerned bus driver came around and asked if he was alright.

'He'll be arlreet mate. It's the drink, it'll kill the pain,' John said to the worried bus driver. 'Haway Gus, let me give yeah a hand marra.' John dragged his mate from under the bus onto the pavement.

'Is his heed ok now, John?' asked Billy and then looking down at Gus and holding two fingers up he quizzed: 'How many fingers have ah got up? Dee you still want to be called an ambulance or are you called Gus?'

Everyone, except the bus driver, who had shaken his head and called them, *Drunken idiots*, laughed and dragged the war wounded ginger casualty to his feet. The bus driver shouted one more obscenity, climbed back in his cab and drove off into town.

'Piss off you bastards. I could have been killed man,' Gus said. 'Me leg hurts like bugger it man.'

'Here, get this down yeah,' John said taking a half bottle of Scotch from his Barbour coat pocket and handing it to the patient.

Gus drank about a quarter, wobbled a bit and handed it back. 'That's better. Where's that baldy bastard gone? See he didn't help.'

'He's off to the match man. You kna what he's like, always manic. And it's worse today, it's the Mags. What the hell would you expect him to be like?'

And indeed, it was the derby again. Marc had not slept for days and had driven over to John's house on the coast for an 8 am start to the treatment for his mania – a barbeque and many, many drinks in February as dawn broke. He wouldn't eat any of the BBQ because John's caring wife gave him his match day bowl of cornflakes while he started on many cans of algae-covered Guinness that had been taken out of the ice covered garden pond. The cans had been in there since the summer BBQ's. Ginger Gus kindly reminded him of that BBQ where Marc had been pushed into the pond by Big Don's temperamental child, Metty. Both were rabid Newcastle supporters which made the humiliation unbearable for the big man. As was the humiliation of his mates' laughter as he chased the little cherub around the garden with a set of hedge trimmers, unable to catch the mocking, much nimbler eleven year old. 'You little black and white bastard! I'll droon yeah if I catch yah.'

Obviously the pain and humiliation were still fresh in the disturbed mind of the big man who was staring at the frozen pond in some catatonic stupor induced by a terrible flash back of his near death drowning at the hands of Metty the Mackem baiter. Recovering from the memory, he went into the kitchen to eat his lucky match day cornflakes while his long suffering kids wearing their full football strips were sent into the house to warm up with a hot dog and coke and to watch the 1973 Cup Final.

The derby day BBQ at John's overlooking the sea was traditional for 12 o'clock kick off derby matches. Pubs were shut and with two or three helicopters flying overhead constantly, police and ambulance sirens and many police cars whizzing along the coast from 8 am, the ambience was not much different to a night out in Beirut and it was outstanding compared to playing normal games. So much so that John always obtained from one his more environmentally touched employees a leg of a freshly slain deer to BBQ. He roasted it whole on the stainless steel BBQ made by one of his other employees from the steel he'd pinched from John. Symbiosis in action you may say. Pieces were cleaved off it with a large axe and were served to those mental enough to eat it; mainly John, Doc Kevin and of course Gus.

As the morning wore on Marc became more worried and paced relentlessly around the garden followed by his two kids who were reciting him details of Sunderland and Newcastle's attendance records and Sunderland past wins. Marc checked these facts by constantly perusing his newspaper cuttings in his wallet.

'John, the fire is dying out and there's nee more charcoal,' Gus shouted over to the host who had taken pity on Marc's two kids following their father pacing around the garden in their football shorts and strip and chased them back into the house out of the freezing cold to read more football programmes in the warmth while his own daughter watched *Little Mermaid*.

John had grabbed Marc in an attempt to counsel him and sat him down on the large rock in the garden. He shouted back to Gus: 'The bait's finished, we can hoy some wood on to keep us warm. I haven't any logs left mind.'

Marc came out of his trance and came up with a solution to the wood shortage.

'I'll chop that black and white's tree down. That'll be a good omen for the match.'

So Marc decided to chop down John's Newcastle supporting TV presenter neighbour's small apple tree that leaned over John's fence using the deer slaying axe. The neighbour was a very nice man who was something of a legend in North East football TV. He had just retired when John moved there. He invited John and Marc in for drinks early days. Strangely, after drinking a bottle of his dust covered Gin John came to realise that he was quite parsimonious with his drinks and as he listened to the curses about his new employer from Marc every time he turned up next door, he never invited them in again. However, this first and only time in his house John couldn't help notice photographs of Sunderland's 1973 FA Cup Final team and personal photographs of him with old players like Charlie Hurley and Len Shackleton dotted around. He did not notice any Newcastle photographs. On querying why he had chosen to work for Newcastle he confessed to them that Sunderland had failed to support him in his efforts to follow a post-retirement career which disappointed him greatly. Newcastle had seen a role for him and for nearly twenty years from then on he worked diligently for Newcastle through the *glory days* of Kevin Keegan, Gazza, Sky, Europe and Sir John Hall.

The residents of that place were always traumatised when he came in and out of the house dressed in Newcastle tracksuits, coats and ties as everyone else around supported the red and whites. He was however a good source of tickets for the derbies and to help any Newcastle supporting friend of John with meetings and photo shoots with Keegan, Shearer, Ginola etcetera: A gentleman, a very nice and helpful man. But sadly Marc couldn't get over the stress of John having a neighbour who had been one of his own tribe and, insanely in Marc's frantic mind, gone over to the dark side. As a result of such angst he was prone to periods of social disorder with the poor neighbour's property.

Luckily, John's wife stopped Marc by battering the BBQ tongs over his back before the tree tumbled. He returned to the rock and stared intensely at the frozen pond, drinking more algae covered cans of Guinness wondering if the black and white tree had been a bad omen for today's match. This mental cruelty abated and he refocused on worrying when his lucky match day bacon, eggs and tomatoes were coming out.

The barbeque fire died out and the helicopters kept flying over the town like those in the old Korean War TV series *MASH*. There were about eight people in the garden who had drunk a Cornish Tin mine's output of fishpond cooled beer. It was now time to stop enjoying themselves and suffer the mental torment and hounds of hell of the derby match. To assist the anxiety treatment, two bottles of whisky were produced for the walk to the match.

So now we know. It was this quantity of booze that was the cause of Ginger Gus's tumble off the pavement under the bus. It was also the cause of the slight altercations after the match yet again with the hordes of Magpies let out of the ground a bit too early. It was also the cause of Marc and John sitting in a pub after the match wondering where everyone was. It took them several minutes and a pint to realise that they were in the wrong pub and also that Marc had lost his kids again. Yes, early morning drinking and Derby day frolics can be bad for your health.

The boys met up in *The Howard Arms*, watching the lost, the lonely and the war damaged arrive. Derby day tales about who had seen, done or been done by the travelling hordes from over the water abounded as with every post derby match drink. Marc was united with his adoring children who consoled him about the defeat by quoting facts and figures about the 9-1 1908 win for Sunderland at St James Park. His besotted daughter tried to cheer him with the old joke about Newcastle's one eyed ex-Chairman, Lord Westwood: 'Heh dad, why does Lord Westwood wear an eye patch?'

Uninterested grunt from Dad while staring wildly into the ether.

'It's so he can put it over his good eye when he watches that black and white shite on the pitch,' answered his angelic daughter, smiling lovingly at her deranged dad awaiting some unrequited affectionate confirmation of his hate for his rivals and his love for her. He hardly heard her in his angst.

'If Leicester beat Southampton and we beat Wolves next week, we'll have twenty-three points,' her father said to Billy, totally oblivious to his daughter's loving attempt to stop him hurling himself off Roker Pier. And then turning to his wallet he pulled out the fixture list and continued his planning for the next match. 'Billy, we play Stoke on Tuesday night after Wolves. I'll pick you up at lunchtime and we'll head down. If we draw with them and the Mags get beat off Arsenal then we'll be one point above the bastards.'

He put his worn fixture list away and sat back worrying about the Wolves match. There was mayhem all around with bodies coming in bloodied up or stressed out, none of which bothered Marc.

Crazy Jim arrived and made everyone but Marc laugh: 'Heh lads, just been in *The Fort*. Some daft bugger came in with a dead seagull under his arm and I'm saying to Paul: *'This bloke isn't reet, should be fun this'*. And sure enough he goes off to the bogs and comes back bollock naked and pushes in to the bar to get a drink.'

Everyone chuckled at the thought.

'Aye, mental but that wasn't the funny bit,' Jim continued.

'Seems funny to me, the daft twat,' Billy commented.

'No, what was funny was he was wearing the seagull as a hat wrapped around his head. The barmaid looked at the daft bugger, shrugged her shoulders in despair and said, *For ****'s sake, not you again.*'

'There are some weird buggers about on derby day,' John said smiling.

'I heard he was from Shotton Colliery,' Jim remarked.

'That'll be reet,' said Ginger Gus. He worked with lots of Durham pit lads and knew the score.

'Talking of seagulls I once went to a Hartlepool versus Darlington derby,' John interjected. 'My mate Sean from Darlo caught a live seagull after the match and hid it in his coat. Why, he never said. I guess he was just crackers and pissed and thought it a good laugh. He and his mad mates were heading back on the train without tickets and as the train was heaving with nutters they never thought the guard would come around checking. Anyway one brave guard did. He asked Sean for his ticket and he opened up his coat and the terrified bird shot out and pecked the guard on his lip. The bird wouldn't let go. Sean held it by two hands tugging it as the guard jumped and howled trying to pull it off his lip. The bird still wouldn't let go. The guard is screaming and everyone laughing and creating mayhem, Sean still has the bird by his two hands standing on his seat falling over everyone as the guard is shaking his head and clawing at the bird's head, blood pouring down onto his uniform.'

The crowd in the bar are howling, by now imaging the scene.

John takes a drink and concludes the tragic avian tale: 'Eventually the bird lets go and the guard falls to the floor. Sean stuffs the poor creature back in his jacket and the train pulls into Darlo station. The lads do a quick runner leaving the poor guard with some more considerate human beings who were stemming the blood from his upper lip. Sean told me he kept the bird for ages in his hen hutch and fed it bread. Again he never said why and I never asked - he's not reet in the heed as you may guess.'

Ginger Gus confirmed this again: 'Aye, that'll be reet. Nivva met anyone from Darlo who was arl there.'

John continued with his Darlington tale.

'He used to be a naughty boy did Sean. He and his mates were banged up for fighting after the match and hauled before the court. He told me a funny story about it like the seagull one in a way. Seems the Magistrate was giving each of his mates' heavy fines and then allowing them to pay five pounds a week and when he came up in front of the beak fined him seventy pounds at five pounds a week for breach of the peace. Sean pleaded could he pay only two pounds week? The lady magistrate asked why as he was a welder on great money at Cleveland Bridge. Sean said he replied in complete innocence and meaning what he said and not taking the piss: *Its coz I'm saving up for the Blackpool weekend.* The court erupted in laughter with the lads in the gallery shouting. *She didn't find it funny at all,* Sean said morosely to me, *She made me pay ten pound a week the old bastard.'*

Crazy Jim laughed. 'Did I tell you about a similar story?' and not waiting for an answer he told his own story of court appearances: 'Aye, had some fun in court. We were up before the beak and one of the lads was charged with assaulting an officer of the law – a police dog! He'd bitten the bugger, ha ha. The beak asked him why he bit it. He replies: *Well he started it. He bit me first.* The court room went crazy with laughter.'

'Brilliant – arrested for biting a police dog. That was a bit 'ruff'. Bet he was barking mad,' Gus said making everyone chuckle at the puns and then one more one liner. 'Did he get to walkie out after the uproar?'

'Nah, sadly the magistrate didn't find it funny; banged up again. But I managed to get a decent beak and get off one other match when really I shouldn't. I'd laid out some Sheffield hoolies who jumped me and my teenage nephew. The poliss arrested me and as they took me cuffed to the station I complained bitterly as the others had been the aggressors. Do you know what the bugger told me?'

'Nah - come on, what?' Billy asked.

'That they only arrest the winners,' Jim answered the lads chuckling at the humour and the perversity of the men in blue. He continued, 'But I managed to outwit the bastards in court. I claimed that as the aggressors had attacked an innocent father and his nephew, I, as a licensed security man, had acted within the law and by restraining them, that is knocking them out, I'd made a citizen's arrest. It seems the magistrate liked that legal argument. I was acquitted.'

'Aye that'll be reet,' Ginger Gus said sarcastically. 'Three sparked out and you claim self defence. Surprised yeah didn't have yeah gun with yeah Jim?'

'I didn't have it those days. Didn't bring it today, chances of being lifted at a derby are high. Mind you a few months ago I pulled it out at an Oldham night match when their lads spotted me, Stan and Paul in their end and started to surround us. They ran like hell when I pulled it out and pointed. The funny thing was the police didn't confiscate it but moved us into the paddock. You win some you lose some with the law. Had a laugh later mind nearer home; I was driving the van back and spotted three lads walking home from a night out. I stopped the van and pulled on the balaclava and leaped out à la SAS with gun and shouted: *Get down you bastards! On the floor!* The terrified lads fell to the floor. I was standing above them gun pointing at them and shouted. *Don't ******** move you bastards!* But one of them moved his hand to his jacket and to inside pocket. *I told you not to move!* I screamed. The lad turned his head up from the floor, wheezing and with breathing difficulty and pulled out a blue plastic tube from his inner pocket: *I'm only trying to get my inhaler!*'

Crazy Jim took a swig, threw his head back laughing. The team all looked a bit shocked at this one, even Ginger Gus, but Jim just laughed through it all and concluded the sorry medical tale: 'I felt sorry for the lad mind, told him not to worry it was a mistaken identify and jumped back in the van. Aye, you had to laugh.'

Ginger Gus turned to a yet again a very shocked young Keith: 'Towld yeah didn't ah? He's not reet man.'

Marc, oblivious to the asthmatic's fate or anything else, stood up and said to his two children who were thumbing through the match day programme for Sunderland's results and next fixtures: 'Haway! Yeah mother is picking us up at *Blockbusters*. Those black and white bastards are either locked up now, in hospital or gone back to their dark lands and I need me tea - me guts are ganning mental after arl this. How yeah's can laugh and joke and drink ah'll nivva kna. It's Stoke next and we need the points.'

And indeed, it was Stoke and more fun to be had.

CHAPTER SIXTEEN
Port Vale, Stoke and Ripping Yarns

The lads drove down to Stoke and attempted to get into a pub before the police closed them or the pubs were taken over by home fans. This was as a result of past experience in the Potteries which could be pretty lively for a place that makes china tea-pots. Port Vale is one of those places you had no idea where it was until you had to go there. Its only claim to existence was when Len Martin and then Tim Gudgin read out on BBC television the classified football results from the teleprinter on Saturday teatime: *'Port Vale nil...Tranmere one'*.

And where the hell was Tranmere? Well as the years and misery rolled on these became normal away venues for the tormented lads.

Port Vale on a cold Tuesday night wasn't high on the must do bucket list of things for anyone, but Ginger Gus, John and Manic Marc decided it was better than work so why not take a day off and go down and try it.

A few early *Tetley* beers in Wetherby on the way down and a take away of some of the world's best fish and chips at *The Wetherby Whaler* for two of them and a lucky match day bacon, eggs and tomatoes at a cafe up the road for Marc and they were on time for an early afternoon arrival into the pubs. When they arrived about 2.30 pm the police had already realised there were hordes down from the North East and had closed a number of pubs so they walked around searching for one that was open. John spotted the men following them quite early on and mentioned it to his friends. There were about eight men and they were obviously tracking them.

'Best try get into somewhere public like a pub where we can get against a wall and not get isolated and surrounded when it comes to the crunch lads,' John suggested.

'For ****'s sake the way my guts are man and now I have to get stuck into these micey bastards and mebbie miss the match locked up. Dee they not kna there's a match on for Christ's sake. The forst one that comes near me I'll bury the bastard,' Marc grunted, annoyed his match day routine might be interrupted.

They walked a few more yards, turned a corner and ahead of them lay a pub doorway. "What the hell: even if it's full of them, we've a better chance,' John said and they tentatively opened the door while Gus looked back. It was obvious to him that the gang had seen them go in.

As they entered all they could see was a sea of red and white and lads climbing on tables, singing and swinging off the rafters; thirty or so Sunderland crazies all well drunk and happy.

'This should be fun,' said Marc with a smile and the three prey turned and waited behind the door for their predators to be enlightened. The first few burst through the door fully expecting it to be full of Port Vale, their faces a picture when they saw the zoo in front of them.

'Hello lads. Fancy a go now?' Ginger Gus mocked. He picked up a half drunk glass of stale lager and poured it over the first one's head. The rest got stuck in the doorway as the earliest entrants were backing off from the general movement of a red and white wall towards them. They were allowed to scamper back, pushing and jostling each other, out of the doorway and into the holes they'd emerged from.

'We were a bit lucky there marra,' John said to his mate Marc as they settled in to join the happy throng.

'Character building,' was the predictable reply as he thumbed through the fixture list in his wallet.

That evening standing on a bleak grassy knoll watching a dire football game, John felt a bit like those who wonder about the lone gunman on his knoll in Dallas, Texas. *Is this place real or is it a conspiracy to drive me insane?* The only fun was that Sunderland had a player called Agnew who was bald as a coot and Ginger Gus loved taking the piss out of him most matches. He had a special name for him which had wound up people in the past and he was hoping that it would again given how dire the evening had been so far.

'Give the ball to Davett man!' he howled out whenever Sunderland attacked. And when Agnew headed the ball or received the ball he shouted: 'Come on Davett!'

For those you about to observe that Sunderland never had a Davett, well you are correct; so why did the ginger one have fun using the name? Well, he didn't usually need a reason - he lived to take the piss - but this time there was method in his madness. He was a lover of Michael Palin's *Ripping Yarns* and in the episode *Golden Gordon* about a failing Yorkshire team, Barnstonworth United, the key player was the baldy, syrup-wearing village butcher, Davett, who did indeed closely resemble Agnew.

Plainly, unaware of the Palin masterpiece, the man in front became annoyed at Gus's shouts, which of course, was Gus's purpose in the first place anyway. 'He's not called Davett man. It's Agnew,' said the man lured into turning around and correcting a drink induced and wobbly Ginger Gus.

Minutes later the ball went flying over Agnew's head. Ginger Gus cried out: 'Haway man Davett needs a better cross than that man. You couldn't cross a road you! Haway Davett, get stuck in lad!'

The man irritated again turned around. 'Heh man, have you never watched Sunderland before. The man is Agnew. Who the hell is Davett?'

Gus wobbled towards the man, stuck is ginger tash in his face and said: 'He's the best baldy player ivva to have played for Sunlun man. He's playing arl reet the neet tee. Look!' and he pointed at the ploughed field which masqueraded as a pitch.

The man turned away shaking his head. His two mates were suggesting maybe it would better if they moved off.

'Haway man! Manager, bring on Haggerty F. This winger is gash he'll nivva cross to Davett,' howled Gus again.

The man turned around again. 'We don't have a ******** Haggerty F man and we don't have a Davett. Are you alreet in the heed son?'

Marc, uninterested in Gus's japes, was getting chewed with it all now, as time was moving on and the points were slipping way. Annoyed with the distraction he looked down at the man and he hissed through a clenched lipless mouth: 'Aye yeah're reet. The ginger twat isn't reet in the heed. Arlways wasn't - still isn't. But if you don't **** off annoying me and watch the match you won't have a ******* heed to be reet with.'

The man and his two mates decided that they'd move along and away from the Michael Palin appreciation society. All a bit silly really I guess, but have you ever stood at Port Vale freezing your nuts of on a Tuesday night watching Davett play? You'd fancy a laugh too, surely?

What wasn't so silly was the Stoke match. Sadly it started with a very similar tale to the Port Vale stalking one but with a very different outcome. This time they met up with Crazy Jim and a whole couple of minibuses of Sunderland and ended up in a pub near the ground. This is until they realised this just happened to be the main Stoke pub and the whole place goes up. The police arrived with dogs biting everyone and blokes jumping onto the pool table while mayhem reigned all around. Then, through the door bursts a policeman on a horse! A bloody horse in a pub which seemed to calm things down - no one had ever seen a policeman on a horse in a pub before. It was lucky this hadn't been a Newcastle match or the poor horse might have been punched. As it was both Stoke and Sunderland were equine lovers and the warring tribes declared a truce, joined each other in feeding the horse *Paulo Mints'* and the beer flowed again.

Yes, days out in the land of Ming vases and Wedgewood tea-pots were always fun.

CHAPTER SEVENTEEN
Vietnam, Roy Keane, Celtic & Rangers

'Oh, Roy Keane! Velly good, velly, velly good...please go...go please.'

John was attempting to clear immigration at Tan Son Nhat International Airport, Ho Chi Minh City, Vietnam. He had tried this several times during his period of working and living there and it had always been a nightmare. Hours of standing in line while uninterested and unfriendly officials in their green and red uniforms looked into the air, played with their stamps, periodically lifted his passport and glowered menacingly at him. They looked far too much like the revolutionary guards he had to pass through when living in Vietnam's alter ego, China, for comfort. Always it took up to two and a half hours to pass through, always in humid, stifling heat. But today a miracle! After only five minutes of staring at John as if he were a Green Beret infiltrating the Ho Chi Minh trail on a gook hunt the official eventually turned a page on the passport and his eyes lit up.

'Ho! You come from Sunderland?' the man asked excitedly, his face beaming.

'Yes,' John answered. Experience throughout Asia told him to keep any conversation free of sarcasm, humour or anything that may be misinterpreted as derogatory to the use of endangered tigers penis or those poor pangolins you see on daytime telly to assist his own penile function and especially no derogatory remarks about the passport official's nation's top five standing in the list of the world's most corrupt countries.

'Sunderland! Roy Keane. Manchester United. Best team. I now slupport Sunderland!'

He stamped a page as if he had won the lottery and he shouted something to the next guard. All John could understand in the dialogue was, 'Roy Keane'. He stamped another page almost immediately; an event unknown in the history of John's visits as usually he'd have to wait ten minutes at least for another stamp. He waved him to the next guard who was waving him to come with a look on his face of something half way between the usual scowl and a smile. He put his hand out for the passport and turned it immediately to the personal details page and his face beamed. He shouted something to his mate who had now settled back into staring into cyberspace while a very sweaty and anxious Frenchman was standing in front of his kiosk waiting for some form of action. All John could make out was, 'Roy Keane. Manchester United. Sunderland,' and he turned the page over, smiled at John, stamped yet another stamp and spoke the words: 'Oh, Roy Keane! Velly good, velly, velly good Sunderland...please go...go please.'

John couldn't believe the change of attitude. Nowhere in this whole world or his travelled life had he ever had such a reaction to his place of birth. He put the US$20 note back in the wallet that he'd had in the palm of his hand. Seasoned travellers in Asia always carried at least $US50 dollars in hard currency to pay off the immigration stampers, or sometimes the police or customs. It was called survival. However, today he was chuffed. And it confirmed something he'd known for some years living outside the cauldron of UK football - that the Premier League was all that the millions of distant TV supporters watched and really only two teams mattered to most of them – Manchester United and Liverpool. And Roy Keane was a hero to all of them!

Roy Keane joining Sunderland as manager was a momentous occasion for both Sunderland fans and more so I suspect to the hordes of Manchester United plastic fans scattered in the jungles, bars and beaches of Asia because all of a sudden Sunderland were famous! John thought deeply about this as he sat staring at eye level with the Saigon River in the death trap tin can that masqueraded as a river ferry from Ho Chi Minh to Vung Tau. His main place of residence now was Singapore and when he first arrived 50% of that nation was Manchester United, 45% was Liverpool and 5% the current Premier League club that was most popular. At the time that was Chelsea or Arsenal but it would soon shift on to Man City and then periodically in the great dictatorship lots of Barcelona shirts would begin to appear. But Saturday nights the bars, coffee shops and hawker centres were heaving with Asian looking folk in Man Utd or Liverpool shirts. The Manchester

United shop in the prime location among the world famous retail brands on Orchard Road was huge – the biggest club shop John had ever seen.

The fact that this feast of televised soccer was repeated every Saturday night in such unlikely locations as Kalimanatan, Yangon, Mindanao, Pusan and all across the known Asian world and that most would be wearing Man Utd shirts made John think of a plan. The reaction of the two border guards at the airport started John thinking that maybe Sunderland should capitalise on Roy Keane's popularity. Why couldn't we have a shop the size of IKEA on Orchard Road or Tiananmen Square? Rather than a small shed in Jacky White's market.

John had acquired connections to the President of Singapore, and to some extremely wealthy Asian investors. He also had as acquaintances several ex-UK footballers who lived and commentated on TV out in Asia for ESPN and local channels, some of whom were involved in a deal to buy Newcastle at the time. He also knew that the Singapore Government had built a new National Stadium and had been turned down by Man Utd , Liverpool and Arsenal to play the opening game with the Singapore National team.

John believed that a team managed by Roy Keane would attract a massive following of extremely nationalistic and proud Singaporeans and also the government, which could mobilise billions of dollar support, would also look favourably on someone who helped them with the embarrassment of having no famous team play at their new Stadium. This popularity would then roll out all over Asia and hopefully attract the investors he knew were looking very closely at the Premier League. So, in his extreme optimism for once about his team, he came up with a plan to persuade Sunderland AFC to play the Singapore national team and use this as springboard through marketing the Roy Keane's popularity to move their brand and football reputation to a huge Asian market.

Sadly, he never got a reply to his letter to Sunderland AFC's Chief Executive - and the misery went on.

We all know what actually happened: Shiekh Mansour bought a majority stake in Manchester City in 2008 and then Thaksin Shinawatr bought Leicester in 2010; both Premier League winners. Guo Gaungchang, Wolves. Gao Jisheng, Southhampton. Lai Guochuan West Bromwhich Albion.

Meanwhile Ellis Short bought Sunderland.

Who knows what might have happened if John had received a reply and the Singapore Sovereign Wealth fund, currently third largest in the world, had invested? In the event, nowt changed except they fell to the third division and once Roy Keane had buggered off, John never got through an airport as fast again.

John was constantly amazed at the number of people who watched the Premier League across Asia and how in the strangest places you could bump into ex-patriot supporters of many teams sitting at midnight in a jungle bar with a few locals dressed in their strips of many colours, Leeds, Wolves, Southampton, Partick Thistle and many, many more. The locals would be in their Man Utd or Liverpool or Arsenal counterfeit tops alongside the ex-pat drunken lunatics howling and screaming at the screen, oblivious to the fact that the locals had no sectarian or tribal hatred of opposition teams, towns or countries. Often there would be enclaves of supporters who had settled in various places and the bar would be a shrine to their club.

Thailand was one place where many ex-pats had settled and John's experience was that there were quite a few Newcastle supporters who had taken up bar opening as a new occupation with their new girlfriends. Indonesia was another place, wild in parts and very different to the order and control of Singapore. Which brings me to Batam Island.

On Batam few people could hear you scream. It was a wild place indeed in those days and the people on it were mainly throwbacks to the American Wild West or ZZ Top lookalikes. Let's put it this way, Burt Reynolds turned it down as location for Deliverance. It had a bar called *The Red Cock In* (note the missing *n*) - at the time run by a Glasgow Rangers diehard - also a bar with a huge Newcastle Union Jack and once there was *Rosie's*, with its own double bed for its patrons, a bar owned by an old Sunderland Vauxie.

When John was there the main workforce were deranged American rednecks, perverted Australian bushmen or Magpies. He was tortured continually by his fellow North East chums. Many exiled Newcastle fans survived there and his life was made a misery most days and nights. But one night he decided to strike back. Mickey from South Shields asked him to stay over after the working week on Saturday as the Toon lads were all meeting up on the fourteenth floor of the Melia Hotel for food and booze and a party to watch Newcastle play Manchester United.

'Aye', John said. 'Of course I would' and promptly took the boat home.

Friday night he was out drinking as usual in his emporium of Glasgow Rangers' bigotry *The Sportsman's* with a neighbour from his condo. He was a Yank and he invited John over for the weekend to play golf in Batam. John declined the offer but mischievously thought he could get one over on Mick and the lads. He found out that his American neighbour was to stay in the Melia hotel so he suggested that he should go and see *my mates* on the fourteenth floor and they would look after him. He told him there was a football match on and he'd enjoy that as he'd never watched one.

And John continued to explain to his innocent American soccer virgin: 'You'll need a football shirt though. I'd hate you to stand out, Brad. When we go home pop into the condo and I'll give you a red and white shirt to wear. You'll see all the lads there in the bar watching the TV. They'll be wearing black and white for fun. Just go up to them point to your strip and tell them that red and white is the best colour and the best team in the world. They'll love the banter and the joke. We're like that where we come from. We all love to see each other's team do well.'

'Boy that sounds a hoot buddy. Can you write that down for me John, so I get it right?' And John did.

The next night John was sitting in a karaoke bar and Manic Marc rang from the UK:

'Have you heard the score? Man U - one nowt up: *******
magic."

A few minutes later he rang again.

'Two nowt now - the mags are *******' and then after another
fifteen minutes: 'They are stuffed, three nowt. Ah've nivva been so
happy.'

The next phone call was from Batam: 'You Mackem bastard!
We've got your mate dangling out of the window by his feet. I
couldn't believe it. We go one nowt down and then two nowt and
then just as those Manc bastards score three - I couldn't think it
could get worse - when in waarks an idiot with a Mackem shirt on.
There are fifteen of us arl in black and white. He looks at us and
waarks towards us. I couldn't believe what I was seeing. I then got
a sweat on and thought, *Is this idiot a Mackem suicide bomber?* – (at the
time Batam had been recently attacked by Indonesian Islamic
jihadists and the Bali Bomb massacre had also involved friends of
the lads so they were on high alert). This gormless idiot came
straight over, pulled at his shirt and said, *Howdy folks. This is the best
shirt and team in the world.* For ****'s sake John, I saw arl the lads'
faces and I thought *he's deed* and then I guessed, it's YOU who sent
the daft American twat, and I stopped the lads braying him. I
bloody knew it was you - you Mackem twat.'

John laughed and laughed and Mick then howled down the
phone:

'It's four nowt now! You bastard, this Yank and that Mackem
shirt have cursed us you bugger. They'll drop him for sure now.'

'Now, now Mick calm down, the Yank is innocent and knows
not what he does. Don't drop the poor lad. Mind you if it gets to
five nowt and you drop him will you clean the blood off the shirt?'

'Bugger that! It's getting burnt.'

And it was. The bastards couldn't take a joke!

John was sitting in *The Sportsman's Bar* the next day after the
American Mackem Suicide Bomber Incident reciting the tale to his
drinking partners and had to explain to the more normal of his
friends what it was all about.

The rivalry between Newcastle and Sunderland is a lot like that of Celtic and Rangers in that it had little to do with actual football. In the North East it is a more diffuse and sometimes controversial explanation. Some believe it started in the English Civil War when the City of Newcastle supported King Charles the First and later on would not support the Scottish Jacobite risings but supported King George. Hence, they were called Geordies while Sunderland supported the Parliamentarians and the Scots.

Another convention has it that the original Geordies were miners from Felling coal pit. After an explosion in 1812, George Stephenson invented the *Geordie* lamp named after him which ended up being used more than the Humphrey Davy Lamp in the North East, so all North East miners were nicknamed Geordies. Otherwise they might have been called Humphries. Now that's a thought!

The origin of the term *mackem* is also disputed. One side believes it stems from the accents - people from Tyneside say *mek* and *tek* while people from Sunderland say *mak* and *tak*. The other side believe it stems from an old shipbuilding custom and whether you *make* or *take* a ship. It seems Sunderland shipbuilders could *mak* a ship. Trivial I know, but whole wars have started over less. Look at the Schleswig Holstein Question – bugger all compared to *makem* or *takem*.

More recent than the English Civil War, workers on Tyneside in England, like a lot of areas, were pretty militant and also could be parochial and xenophobic. Tyneside wouldn't let workers from Sunderland (less than nine miles away) work in their shipyards. They'd strike at the blink of Jimmy Hoffa's concrete eye. Parochially, this is put down to hatred referencing the two football teams. In reality most of the hatred was pure job protection arising from a territorial hierarchy bordering on tribalism.

John explained these tenets of North East religion to his assembled throng in the widely Glaswegian sectarian Singapore bar and remembered a tale that he'd heard - a wonderful, tragic but comic example of this tribalism which related to race. He told this story to Denis and his friends in the bar.

'George was a Dr Barnardo's boy (an orphan who was taken into the care of this charitable organisation) and along with his sons, grew up in one of the hardest areas of Sunderland, Hendon Docks. Marvellous man, husband and father but hard as nails. He had to be, he was black and there weren't many black lads in Sunderland. Early days he'd found prejudice was rife in this corner of England. This wasn't such a surprise as when he grew up the only black person his peers had seen was their father when he came back from the pit covered in coal dust.

'When George first worked on the Tyne he faced so much prejudice. They used to drop welding rods on his head. They spat at him, his car was trashed and he was attacked by a couple with a baseball bat after work in the car park. His mate on hearing the story sympathised with his friend: *Aye, Geordie, I'm sorry to hear that son. It must have been hard being black, mate?*

'His reply his friend should have anticipated: *Hadaway man, you daft bugger! It wasn't coz I was black, they had nee bother aboot that man. It was coz I was a Mackem.*'

Thankfully, racism, homophobia, and other forms of harassment and discrimination have been to some extent hounded out of football, and gradually out of society as a whole. As we all know if we have followed football over sixty years this hasn't always been the case but for me and my experience, most of the stuff thrown at players and fans by my acquaintances was done in a perverted sense of fun. Some wasn't correct but most was done in the innocence of ignorance. Black players were rare those days, as they were in our communities, and any small difference in a player, be it colour, hair, size, weight, marital problems, sexuality, you name it, could be fair game. Was it correct? Well, no, obviously not in this more enlightened and multi-cultural world. But we were massively ignorant of other people who didn't fit into our own parochial culture. And I firmly believe we mocked, took the piss and joked out of ignorance, fear of the unknown and pure tribalism - rather than malice.

Then we grew up.

Geordie's story is an example of humour which might be on the unacceptable edge now but tells a true story immersed in

North East Culture. Another example was when Marc was talking to Daft Billy and reminiscing about how to behave with other colours, shapes, sexualities and faiths. One of his tutors at college was asking about his experience of multi-culture and his attitudes to it. When he was at school in Washington, he told the astonished tutor, the whole school had no people of colour and he had never met anyone who wasn't from his area and his colour. Except he told his tutor: 'There was one strange lad who was mocked as he was different.'

The tutor suggested that maybe this was a form of nascent discrimination and abuse.

'Nah, he supported Middlesbrough. He was weird. Neebody supported them.'

I have to add one more example of past racist ignorance and innocence. Paul's dad took him to the match every week. The team had signed their first coloured player. His father was a solid family man, a non-drinking pitman. Bless him - he genuinely believed that the player was from Africa and his knowledge of that diverse continent was limited. When the player missed his first simple goal opportunity in his team's colours, Paul's dad in his naivety (well let's be kind and say it was naive) turned and said: 'If he's not used to wearing byuts, he should take them off and play.'

I'll leave it at that.

And in Singapore John was beginning to understand that actual football was not the problem in The Dear Green Place that was Glasgow, European City of Culture – it was ethnic and religious division. Colour was massively divisive, but not the colour of a person's skin, but his country's flag or fraternity. Here the old religious divides between Scottish Protestants who made up the majority of Ulster's early population and the Catholic Irish who migrated to Scotland, were manifested through support of Rangers or Celtic. This was pure hatred in some cases and in a few old-school dinosaurs, pure bigotry. Like attitudes and behaviours to racism and homophobia in the general football world, *The Dear Green Place* has become more enlightened in its green, blue or orange phobia. Or so you will be told by many of each tribe, and we can thank whoever's God for that.

So it was in the Singapore bar where John was sitting as there were many great people of both Hun (Rangers) and Timm (Celtic) who could mix together without resorting to cut-throat razors at dawn. However, the only colours in that sanctum were orange and blue and the only flags the Union Jack or the Saltire. This was Glasgow Rangers territory and Harry was true blue. The bar was home to the Rangers supporters of Asia and the David Cooper Memorial Society. Often visited by *dignitaries* from Ibrox and Glasgow, it was an oasis for all peripatetic Rangers fans travelling in Asia on business or pleasure.

Harry, who owned the bar, had left Glasgow many years before.

'I left in a hurry, son.'

This was the only thing he had told John about his past life. Many of the characters John had met in Asia seemed to have *left in a hurry* their last place of abode.

One of Harry's best friends and part owner of the bar was one of the leading criminal barristers in Scotland and he came to *The Sportsman's* every year for Burns Night, where he fondly liked to greet the assembled guests of Harry with: 'It's good to see so many old clients in the room.'

With this de facto evidence, I leave us to reflect on Harry's past life.

Harry was what you would call a character. He was a wealth of information on real contracting, sociology, history, poetry, criminology and the past bigotries of Glasgow. John learned a lot about life in late-night conversations with Harry. These conversations would sometimes take place to the sound of a flute and the melodic thump of the Lambeg drum, the sound of Orangemen on a march down a Glasgow or a Belfast street as like-minded patrons would take up the tune of *The Sash* or some other subtle homely Orange tune. Most non-Scots felt strangely out of place on these occasions – and sometimes very confused.

John too was confused. Well, so would anybody. He tried to rationalise these profound tenets of Scottish culture and see some rational sense in it all. Recalling Harry's summary of it all, which I quoted in the introduction to this book, '...*that the real national*

anthem is, to many of our Scottish Rangers loyalists, 'God Save the Queen',
and the country flag is the Union Jack. They are British. Just as the Irish
Tricolour is the flag to our Celtic hosts and they are Scottish,' didn't help
John's confusion.

Luckily, John thought, normal people in Singapore had only to
drink with these people. Paranoid schizophrenia was not what he'd
signed up for during his extracurricular enjoyment. But every now
and then, some normal people might have to work with Scottish
people and then it was only sensible to try to align with their
culture rather than face a *Glasgow Kiss* or a razor across your chops.
He proposed to publish a bit of friendly advice one day for non-
Glaswegians. They could take it or not, but if not best to avoid
attending Ibrox stadium wearing your crucifix and singing quaint
Irish folk songs, and to avoid Celtic Park with bowler hat, sash and
drum.

John was to become hypnotically drawn into these
conversations over many a night and gradually gained a Master's in
The Religious History of Great Britain and Ireland and learned
something very profound which was that whilst they might hate
each other, they still didn't like the English. This was strangely
reassuring, because like Pavlov's Dog, he'd been conditioned to
believe this was a universal constant and it was comforting to
know that despite their own bigoted, psychopathic dislike of each
other – they hated the English more!

Denis was a Partick Thistle fan who drank with John. However,
he was not confused about all this as he had been weaned on
sectarian division in the tough Glasgow streets. He was from
working-class stock, born and bred in the poverty of Glasgow.
You were brought up to be hard. Work hard, play hard. Men were
men, and women were mainly your mothers. As a young man he
went all over Scotland to watch Partick Thistle. I feel that Partick
Thistle fans will enjoy this book as they're a team I'd add to the
misery pot. They too have followed a path of 'relentless misery'.
The Jags won the Scottish cup in 1921. They won the Scottish
League Cup some fifty years later in 1971 (beating Celtic 4-1 in the
final), so Jags fans are long overdue some silverware fifty years on.
The fact that they are currently in the Scottish First Division (the

third tier in Scottish Football) means that it is unlikely to be a major trophy! But as I edit this book, they have won the league! The longest journey starts with one step...

After John had told the Geordie and black Mackem story Denis chuckled and said he could trump that one from Glasgow. It seems Rangers were returning from a European match. Basil Boli (a black player who had just been signed) was stopped at immigration on his return to Glasgow, and was asked all sorts of questions - Where did you come from? Why are you visiting Scotland? Have you got a visa? When he eventually cleared customs and immigration he started complaining to his team mates that he was only being picked on because he was black. Ali McCoist, who was known for his quick wit) said: 'It's nothing to do with being black – it's because you're a catholic!'

As if on cue to finish off this tribal, racist, religious nonsense, the conversation was interrupted when into the bar came a huge man, plainly well sizzled. As he entered he stripped off a Glasgow Celtic football top and waved it at the assembled masses. Earlier in the evening there had been a Glasgow Rangers versus Glasgow Celtic Derby match, -something that resembles a Palestine v Israel kickboxing match, and clearly this man was enjoying the Celtic win. His huge stripped body was emblazoned with Celtic and Irish regalia tattoos; shamrocks, Tricolours etcetera. Draped around his neck were enough gold crucifixes to have converted the whole of the Inca nation. He proceeded to shake hands with everyone and to abuse Harry and any other Hun he came across. Curiously, no one was offended; there was no attempt at physical violence. The size of him and the mad look in his eyes seemed to put most off. This went on for some time until he fell off his stool, mortal drunk, and split his head open and lay there bleeding profusely. Denis, who was standing drinking with Harry, had observed this behaviour with an air of disdain, and whispered to him: 'Are you nay going to help him?'

'**** him! The Fenian bastard,' Harry snarled out of the side of his mouth.

Sharon, his lovely head hunter wife from Borneo, helped him up and mopped up the blood with a dirty beer towel. Denis whispered to John that her nursing skills in the jungles of Borneo had come in useful. They placed the big man on a stool and poured him another Tiger beer to ease the pain and hopefully kill the tetanus or rabies acquired from the bar towel. Surprisingly, given his outburst, Harry went over to him and began to talk and laugh with him. Both of Harry's guests were confused again. Denis asked Sharon: 'I thought Harry wouldn't care about him, he's a Tim (Celtic supporter).'

'Nah,' she said. "He's his best friend from home, Big Tam, and they love each other.'

So they were introduced to male bonding Glasgow style and to Big Tam the Tim, and got very drunk in his company as he told tales of football and days gone by in the Auld Country. John left even more confused over the cultural divide that was Scotland.

Not everyone in the bar was involved in this sectarian rivalry. There were plenty of normal football fans, like Denis, and from all over the world many others, Americans, Aussies, Dutch, Norwegians etcetera who liked strange games like rugby, baseball, tennis, Australian Rules Football, etcetera. John drank and socialised with most of them, the common thread being that all of them were praying, if they had a God, that their projects, huge day rate earnings and debauched expatriate life would perpetually overrun. And consequently, that their life in the Rivendell of the third world would never end. Of course they were all delusional most of the time because one day they would all have to return to the misery of a cold January night standing at Firhill, Celtic Park and Ibrox dreaming of the glory days of 1921.

CHAPTER EIGHTEEN
Reading, Wigan, Fire Engines & Hot Dog Stands

Travelling can have great benefits as we all knew before the virus hit but sometimes *the foreigners* take advantage of the poor visitor; especially when they travel in thousands and always participate ravenously in the local cuisine and epicurean feasts on offer. Crazy Jim was often such a participant in sampling the delights on offer at various locations. Moreover like the huge bodied food critics on *Masterchef* he could also be very cynical and disparaging at the service and price inflation on offer. Most Saturdays the arrival of the hordes from the North amongst the rolling council houses and pubs of the Thames Valley provided happy hunting grounds for rapacious landlords and vendors when they arrived to watch their team against Reading; but sometimes the local greed came back to haunt them. And so it was with Crazy Jim and a landlord who thought he was cleverer than the master.

Crazy Jim and his mates had arrived early doors for the match without tickets and placed themselves in the pub waiting for supporters of both clubs to come in and hoped to secure spare tickets. After a couple of pints they got hungry and one of them went to the bar to find out what sandwiches were on offer. He was told by the landlord that the pub didn't do food. One more pint and Crazy Jim went to the bar to order the next round. Scanning the bar and surroundings he spotted a huge pile of sandwiches covered in cling film. Chuffed that his mate must have been mistaken about no food, or that the landlord had responded kindly to the lads' hunger, he asked for eight of any variety the landlord's made and half a dozen bags of crisps with them.

'Home fans only,' the landlord said, grinning and looking very satisfied with his answer.

Jim, shook his head and grunted to himself, thinking, *Well that's not very friendly is it you lying bastard,* and returned to the table, watching the landlord carefully for any sign of weakness. He kept his conversation with the landlord and knowledge of the existence of the sandwiches to himself. Soon the Reading supporters trooped in and the grinning landlord began serving them drinks and a sandwich. Jim kept looking over, pondering the next move. It was obviously best that they headed off to the ground to collar the hundreds of Sunderland supporters now arriving on the coaches. The lads made a move to drink up and go but Jim said: 'Sit tight lads. I need to have a chat with the landlord.'

He strolled through the crowd to the bar and as the landlord came over he explained that as the pub was becoming full it would be best to double up and ensure they managed a couple more pints before they had to go. Furthermore, he explained to the landlord: 'The lads are struggling with the local beer mate. I know it's pricey but can you fill us eight pints of Guinness please?'

'Sure. We don't often get people buying eight pints of this stuff in one go. It'll take a little while to pour mate. You got the time ok?'

'Yeah, no worries mate.'

Jim stood and laughed and chatted to landlord about the match and the ambience of his pub as the landlord carefully poured the precious Irish fluid. 'We've enjoyed it in here. Don't often get the welcome you gave us when we came in. We'll remember it,' Jim said as the landlord was finished and diligently placed the eighth pint next to the seven other perfectly poured pints, Jim said: 'Great pints them. Do you like Guinness?'

'Nah mate, I hate the stuff.'

Jim turned to the lads and nodded for them to get ready to leave and looked the contented man in his eyes with his own manic stare and broke the silence with: 'Well that's a shame. You'd better sell them to your home fans...only.'

He turned and walked away, leaving the landlord catatonic and staring at the crazy man's back. Feeling happy at last, Jim put his hand on the shoulder of one of his mates and they formed a chain each with a hand on the next's shoulder. Jim waved goodbye to the still shocked landlord and they trooped out of pub singing: 'Hi Ho, Hi Ho, it's off to work we go!'

Snow White gave Dopey the landlord a cuddle.

WIGAN ATHLETIC

Wigan in 1988 was famous for one thing - mud. Not the mud on the pitch or the shirts and shorts of the players but the mud on the fans. And no, they didn't invade the pitch this time. They created football's biggest and best mud slide on the terrace.

The game was another near end season cruncher. Wigan were chasing the play offs and Sunderland the Championship, which they actually won. The crowd was a sell out. Most Sunderland fans were in the away end which was known as *the Shevvy End*. Really it should have been known as *the Ploughed Field End* because that's what it was except for a few terrace steps at the end wall. One wonders how it was allowed post-Taylor report but sure enough it was and provided much fun to the Sunderland revellers uninterested in the match as they slid down the mud bank on their backs, tummies, and arses, one lad performing an Olympic winning double somersault and it's all on YouTube for you to watch.

Great day out for all but difficult for the mudslide participants to get a pint afterwards or a lift home as most landlords, bus drivers and car drivers were not amused at the soaked, mud covered hippos who arrived drenched at their doors. But the fun of the Olympic gymnasts and the *Cool Running* tobagganists (do you like that one? Lads sliding covered in brown mud, Olympic Jamaican tobbagan team movie - good link?) is not the point of this story. It's about purveyors of refreshment ripping off the fans. However, in another clever link, it all started because of the mud slide.

Manic Marc was standing next to a hot dog stand which was on top of the hill where the mud slide was and behind the fans. He thought the food was pricey for a town and ground like Wigan. He felt strongly that a great working class area famous for the Casino, a pier and Northern soul shouldn't have prices like that. The prices were displayed on the van like the half time football scores were displayed on the scoreboard at the back of the Roker End years before and how cricket scores still are in most grounds. They were chalked on metal squares hung on hooks. Daft Billy decided to lift the squares up and see what was underneath and sure enough the real normal prices for normal away fans were fixed and firm on the board underneath - half the price the vendor was charging for Sunderland. This annoyed the two men greatly. But providence and the Devil can strike at any time. And, maybe it was the rain over the last few days that had made the mud slide for the fans on the terrace or maybe it was the stamping and clapping of thousands of fans that caused the vendor's van to begin sliding down the hill at the back. Who knows now? We'll never know. But sadly, for the vendor, his van somehow seemed to become unstable and slowly it started to slide down the hill, finally toppling over with its contents flying off into the air and mud. With such bad luck, one wonders if he or she learnt their lesson that *cheats never prosper*. Well, certainly when the daft lads are around they don't.

SOMEWHERE IN THE MIDLANDS

At one match in the Midlands it was also damp but soon became damper but great fun as bonfire night started early that year. The lads were enjoying a few beers before the game in a pub some way off the ground. A lad in the pub was getting restless because as at Reading and Wigan the landlord had put the beer prices up to fleece the visiting fans yet again. This price fiddle was bugging this stranger a lot the lads were to hear a bit later. Which is understandable as things like that can really bug you.

After some time Crazy Jim, who been observing the stranger, as he does, said to the lads: 'Let's get out of here I'm sure that maniac is going to kick off soon over the beer prices and I have to pick up some tickets down the road and can't afford to get banged up.'

Marc looked at his watch, panicked: 'Only time for one more, the match kicks off soon. Haway, let's tilt.'

Of course there was plenty of time and a couple of lads protested but they headed towards another pub. They walked about half a mile and as they approached the next pub several fire engines hurtled past with their sirens screaming out. Standing in the new pub they spotted the group with the same dissident lad who had been restless about beer prices before and Crazy Jim ended up in the toilet talking to him. Even though they were used to Crazy Jim's antics, he came back with an astonishing tale.

'I was talking with that lad over there, the one who was kicking off before. I asked him what his problem was. It seems he just doesn't like Sunderland supporters being ripped off. So you'll nivva guess what he reckons he did?'

'Come on you mad bugger. You'll tell us anyway,' said Gus.

'He set the pub alight! That's the fire engines that we saw.'

'Dear God, that's a bit ower the top, isn't it?' young Keith blurted out, shocked yet again.

'Aye, it is,' answered John. 'Where's the nutter from Jim? Southwick, Hendon or somewhere?'

'Seems he's flown in from Europe somewhere, I think it might be somewhere on the Mediterranean, mebbies Algeria I think he said. He lives there now.'

'By hell, we've met some truly weird people supporting the lads Jim,' John said.

'Oui, certainement; on fait, Jean,' said Crazy Jim, surprisingly fluent in French.

That's something he'd kept quiet John mused. *It never ceases to amaze me who you meet following this lot.*

CHAPTER NINETEEN
Swindon, Charlton, Playoffs & Chicken Madras

THE NEWCASTLE PLAYOFFS

To get to Wembley yet again to play Swindon in the final, they had to play Newcastle and Marc and John had to face someone more frightening than the four Chelsea lads - Gus's wife. She was the only one he was afraid of and the only one who kept him in check; a frightening woman to Gus and to his mates, as she seemed to be able to freeze most of them with just one stare. Outside of managing Gus's behaviours she was a very successful and caring person with small children and we can guess that was great experience for managing Gus. And on that one night she really needed those skills.

So it was the semi-final playoffs for promotion from the second division to the first - Newcastle v Sunderland, a momentous occasion. John had been in Corsica on business with a client whom he gradually realised was Don Corleone's cousin and who had held him captive in an armed villa and it had seemed highly unlikely he'd make it to the match. Marc had vowed at his dad's funeral never to spend a penny in St James Park so he wouldn't go and Gus didn't have a ticket either so John arranged with George Taylor , the ex-TV sports presenter to get three tickets in the Newcastle seats for Crazy Jim, Paul and Stan, instantly regretting he'd done so.

Crazy Jim, Stan and Paul went to a pub near Central Station early. It was heaving with Newcastle. They kept their heads down and talked with the locals as if they were part of the same tribe. The assembled Magpies sang and called out what damage they would do to the arriving lads from Sunderland and kept drinking waiting for the trains to arrive from Sunderland. The trains duly arrived and the police arranged the escort to the ground. As the escort approached the pub the Newcastle lads ran into the doorway. Crazy Jim leapt up from his usual strategic position at the back way out of the pub in case it really kicked off prompting Paul and Stan to jump up with him. He noticed through the windows that at the front of Sunderland was a mob of known lunatics and psychopaths from East Durham covered by hordes of Northumbria's finest with rabid dogs (not the fans by the way, but actual police dogs). The crazy man and his two mates shouted from the back: 'Get the ******** Mackems!' and began pushing Newcastle boys out of the pub doorway. Some of the front line were very reluctant, others weren't, but the Newcastle crazies urged on by the three traitors at the back pushed and ejected their *forlorn hope* right into the paths of the rabid police dogs, the rabid Frankie's army's pit boots and the police truncheons.

'Get into them! The red and white bastards,' the crazy man howled as he stood at the back and pushed the crowd out into the maelstrom.

Stan, always the sensible one, said: 'Let's get out afor this turns nasty,' and they ran out of the back door that Jim, experienced in pranks and jolly japes like this, had always known was their way out if it kicked off. They ran into the back of the Sunderland escort and joined the red and white horde. Then, as they walked past the same pub, they gesticulated at those remaining howling Magpies who had not caught rabies or were dazed by the police truncheons. A few of the Newcastle mob recognised them and they screamed out and tried to climb over the police at them: 'You Mackem bastards! You were with us arl day in here...'

Crazy Jim and his friends just smiled and walked on with the hordes into a night of even more horror, fun and comedy.

John had given up on getting home and had given his ticket to his nephew. To his surprise his company paid his ransom and he managed to escape his captor and took a flight on the day of the match from Nice; too late to sort the match but he arranged to get into Sunderland about 3 30 pm to meet Marc and Ginger Gus. He bought a litre bottle of *Pernod* at Duty Free to give to Gus who loved the French aniseed water of intoxication and he got quietly sizzled in Business Class. He took a taxi from Newcastle Airport to Sunderland and they drank solidly from the later part of the afternoon. Ginger Gus had told them their lass was out that night and he'd made a curry and put it in the slow cooker all day, so why not go back to the house and put the match on Radio Newcastle? *Why not?* they thought.

Sadly, Gus was not one to take drink well. After several pints he had a propensity to slur and get wobbly and had little control of even more quantities supped; if it was there, and especially if it was free, he'd carry on until extremely happy. And after half a bottle of *Pernod* several beers and a bottle of Asda's best Bordeaux he was a bit wobbly on his legs as he served up the pretty well burnt curry. The match was approaching half time and two of the lads were sitting at the table listening intensely and getting excited although Marc's ulcers were jumping out of his oesophagus with the stress and the curry. Gus was looking more and more like he was in another world slurring his words. John was worried about what might happen to marital bliss and asked Marc: 'When's his lass due back? Ah divn't want to be in here when she comes in and see's the clip of him.'

'Late, ah think, after the match. We can bugger off afor she gets in.'

Both men were terrified of meeting Gus's carer.

About five minutes later John thought he heard something outside the room. Ginger Gus was staring blankly at both of his dinner guests, plainly unaware of the sound of the match in the background. He took his glass of red wine and moved it to his lips. He tried to pour it down into his mouth but it dribbled out all down his chin and shirt - just as the door opened. There standing was Gus's darling wife, her face like the fabulous Gorgon's about to turn them all to stone. Gus stared directly at her, the wine trickling out of his mouth down his chin. He tried smile and to speak but gurgled instead and fell face first into his curry.

'You drunken bastard!' the Gorgon howled.

The disgusted lady ran across the room, grabbed her husband's ear and pulled him out of the steaming Madras and yanked him upright. She pulled him by his ear out of the room (years of dealing with the lovely children of Sunderland had made her an expert at discipline of the unruly) and began dragging him up the stairs to bed, slapping him conscious. When she reached the top she shouted down the stairs. 'Wait till I get down there! What did you bastards do to him?'

Marc turned to a terrified John and whispered: 'For ****'s sake lets tilt. Get outta here afor she comes down.'

And they ran out of the back door and ran the next half mile back to the Club to listen to the second half.

Sunderland won. Newcastle invaded the pitch. There was hell on outside the ground. And Marc and John drank till daylight in a lock in.

Ginger Gus slept like a baby in the bairn's room unaware of it all.

SWINDON

We return to the misery of Wembley - Manic Marc's Mausoleum. Great weekend was the Swindon game, a desperate game and result so yet again the trip back home was hell for him. All he ever wanted to do when sat in the front seat of a car, van or minibus was to become Forest Gump. Not to choose a chocolate out of his box of chocolates and accept philosophically what his momma always said to him: '*Forest, life is just a box of chocolates. You never know what you are going to get.*' Marc knew exactly what he was going to get - hours of motorway in front of him with Ginger Gus who was always very happy with his trip out away from work, farting and getting mortal drunk. But Marc couldn't cope with happiness and anyone enjoying themselves after a match. The lads had again been beaten and he had hours to go to next box of Gaviscon and strip of Ativan. No, he just wanted to be Forest Gump so that he could put on his Nike trainers, Sunderland baseball cap and get out of the vehicle and run and run and run...not long after he did just that.

CHARLTON ATHLETIC

Wembley again and Manic Marc and lads drove down at 5 am to get to the Wembley Hilton for 11 am. They took a friend with them who was a doctor, a PhD who also had a nice company Mercedes car which they hijacked. They hijacked their friend's academic title too to help get them into the Hilton Hotel car park and lounge, hoping that when they arrived in such a prestigious car and with such a prestigious driving licence the security, that was always on the hotel car park, would bow to the ancient law of *droit de seigneur* and let them in. Crazy Jim, Paul and Stan had booked a weekend in the hotel and Stan who had the money and the posh car had told Marc to ensure they used his room number to help get them into the car park and through the guards on the reception. The intention was that they would all meet at 11 am and get blooted in the Hotel's lounge.

The only flaw in this cunning plan was there were seven of them in the car and everyone, including the driver would be half pissed when they arrived. This minor point could never deter the excited fools from persuading the security they were upright and decent citizens. However, there was one further flaw, possibly a fatal one - John had told his nephew from Shiney Row, the one who in his youth couldn't tell Liverpool fans from Sunderland, where they were drinking, so things were pretty well bound to well go astray. Nevertheless, the merry men headed down the M1 full of the joys of a beautiful May dawn.

On nearing arrival the Doc told them to hide all the cans and bottles and try to sober up and act sensibly. A difficult thing because there were about fifty cans all stuffed under the front chairs and piled up on the back seat floor and of course Ginger Gus was squashed in the back farting on Daft Billy's leg. He was becoming his usual wind up, nuisance persona, not really grata but non grata, and that didn't bode well. It only needed one of the stalwart enforcers of hotel policy to be different in any way to the norm, and Gus'd start the piss take and that would be the end of any hint of respectability.

Manic Marc had anticipated this and as they pulled up to the security he unravelled his anguished mind, dropped his Indonesian worry beads and spoke for the first time in ages: 'Keep your gob shut you Ginger bastard or I'll stick that bottle of *White Lightning* you're supping up...'

But he couldn't finish because the Doc cut him off. 'Shush Marc, the sunroof's open. Nee swearing or daft antics man...' and he wound the window down as a monster security man leant into the window.

'Good morning mate. Hi I'm Doctor Black. I am meeting a friend, Stan Jones, room 315. I have car spot booked through him,' the Doc said.

Everyone, even Gus, were looking straight ahead and smiling, trying not to disturb the pile of used cans hidden by the jackets and bags piled on them.

'Morning Sir, have you any identification or confirmation from the hotel please?' the guard asked looking at the assembled masses that resembled either the cast of *The Muppets* or *Godfather Two* depending on your post code and life experience

'I have my driving licence if that will help?'

And the Doc handed over his licence and with a huge smile, keeping his mouth shut as much as possible to keep the fumes in, as he'd supped a few cans of Scrumpy Jack. With confidence he didn't have and hoping rank would work, he said: 'As you can see on the licence sir - Doctor Black.'

'But this isn't proof of any hotel booking sir. I have...' said the guard but he was stopped from saying anymore by a huge shout from behind him.

'How man John, we fund ya!'

And five lads ran through the visitors trying to get into the hotel and one pushed the offside guard out the way and stuck his face in the window.

'How man John, what a ******** place London is man.'

Four others piled around the car and John realising it was the *Shiney lads* opened the window. 'Hi Lads, didn't think you'd mak it.' *Why did I tell the daft twats where we were. This is gonna mess the whole thing up.*

One lad leant over the sunroof shouting: 'How man John, how man, yeah'd nivva believe the ******** man. What a shite place London is...look, look...ah've been stabbed.'

And sure enough he was covered in blood from a wound in his arm and his blood was now dripping all over the windscreen and into the open sunroof.

John's nephew howled out, 'We've been fighting druggies' man. Some wor even puffs man. Druggies, darkies and puffs with blades for ****'s sake. They set on us for nowt man. Nowt man. Nivva seen owt like this place man.'

John sat and reflected on his stupidity, *Shiney Row lads in London, always was going to be a tad problematical. I shouldn't have told them.*

Ginger Gus, though, was over the moon to see a couple of his old school mates and opened the back seat door and piled out causing about fifteen cans to roll out onto the feet of the other guard. He looked down at them and then to Gus, who smiled and, causing Marc to hold his head in his hands, said; 'How man what's yeah problem? The lads need a drink on a morning, Dee yeah cockney ******* not like a drink man?'

The guard looked at Taffy sat on the car, blood pouring onto the bonnet whose face was a picture of puzzlement as it always was, as if the world was just too difficult to understand. He looked at John's nephew who was still talking at a hundred miles an hour looking as if he was about to explode with the excitement of being let out of the lost world they came from. The others were standing staring at him. The last time he had seen such a bunch and such malevolent stares was when he'd spent time as a porter in the psychologically disturbed ward of the prison.

He chose his words carefully to rhetorically answer Gus. 'Yes mate we do. Why don't you all take the car into the park and go and meet your friends in the hotel now. Will you put all the cans back in the car please before you go?'

John looked at Marc, who was now covered in Taffy's blood on his shirt and looked as if he was about to burst his last ulcer, and said: 'Dear God, never thowt I'd be glad to see our youn un and his mates. Let's get out before these buggers wise up and call for more help. Come on lads let's get out and get into the hotel.'

As they all walked into the hotel, John used an old jacket to wrap the wounded arm of his fellow villager. The Doc, like the guard next to his side of the car, had said nothing. His mind was numb. He'd never seen such before. He nodded to the guard and took his licence and thanked the guard who smiled insanely at him as if he'd seen a ghost. The Doc put the gear stick into drive and slowly drove down the ramp into the car park.

Crazy Jim and boys were over the moon to see the crew when it piled into the lounge. The more affluent and sane customers were not. The beer and drink flowed continually until Crazy Jim got chewed with the price of the beer. He sent John's brother-in-law out to get some cheaper booze at the off licence. When he returned, much to the disgust of the more refined clientele, Eight Ace cracked a whole two litre plastic bottle of White Lightning and stood on the nicely upholstered seats and drank most of it, coughing some up onto the beautifully woven Axminster carpet. Someone complained and a bouncer came over to have a word. He requested they stop drinking their own booze or he'd confiscate it.

'They divn't pay you enough to try that son,' John muttered through clenched lips.

Again, on refection, they must have employed extremely placid, or sensible, security at the Hilton that day because, after looking around at the motley crew, Taffy's arm still seeping claret onto the nice woven seats, and certainly once he'd looked into the crazed eyes of Jim who has feeling under his jacket for his favourite replacement extendable cosh, the guard must have agreed with John and hurried back to his safe haven near the cold buffet table.

The animals finished off the take away booze, Eight Ace squeezing the last drops out the plastic bottle of his second two litres of White Lightning. The cracking and crunching sounds of the plastic finally tipped Manic Marc over the edge of his personal cliff face of anxiety and gastric bleeding. 'For ****'s sake, stop that noise you brindle heed bastard. It's torning me stomach inside out. I'll stick it up your...'

'Haway Marc, shut the **** up man. Let's tilt...we're on our way to Wembley,' said Ginger Gus, and he grabbed a smart looking lady in an expensive cut red and white twin suit who was leaving her table with her companions.

'Haway, wifey, let's hev a song eh!' and he broke into, *'Kay surra, suura....whativva may be, may be .....'*

'Please put my wife down will you,' a smartly dressed man interrupted the ginger Doris Day.

Gus looked at the man in a puzzled manner and then the woman, slumped against the man and slurred out:'How man, divn't get vexed. We're off doon Wembley wa y man. Mind yeah, son, yor lass with a fyess and legs like that, she'd mak a canny gallower down the pit man.'

Then he fell over the table, spilling drinks over the couple's feet

'Leave the ginger twat,' shouted Marc, as Daft Billy went to help him up. And as the smart man began to complain, Marc whispered: 'He's pissed and daft. Arlways is, arlways was. Me heed's boiling and I need to get to the match and I'll bury yeah if you and that daft ginger twat delay me.'

The man seemed to understand that Marc's red head and face and bulging green eyes were probably a sign of impending apoplexy so he wisely lead his lovely partner off towards the door and the relative sanity of Wembley Way.

What happened to the wounded Taffy or the Shiney lads once they left Wembley nobody knew or cared. Screaming, jumping up and down for over two and half hours luxury in the gallery at Wembley watching the pain of a penalty shoot-out and another defeat took its inevitable toll. John's head exploded during the shoot-out, never to be the same again. Manic Marc after the van reached Watford Gap, stopped it, put on his Nikes and set off like Forest Gump to walk from Wembley to John O' Groats. He was never to be seen again for years. And then suddenly he reappeared for the Portsmouth cup final at Wembley two years ago. They lost yet again. By then manic man was about finished with power walking and took up studying Arabic black magic curses instead.

CHAPTER TWENTY
Everton and Compassion For Your Fellow Man

I have one final tale that makes me chuckle and says it all about the pathos of supporting football and the FAITH, HOPE AND CHARITY of its supporters. I hope it fills you with joy and love for your fellow homo sapiens and closes this narrative with a sense of hope for the human race. If it urges you to get off the sofa and watching football on TV and experience the agony and ecstasy of following your chosen team across the country, well I for one hope to meet you on British Rail one day for a can or two.

The lads had been to watch Everton. It was Manic Marc and his Everton Carlisle claar hammer knitted crew; Don, Jacko, and Mackie. They changed train at Preston station and it was heaving. With nowhere to sit and stand comfortably they forced their way through the train to the baggage compartment and opened the door. It was empty but for one lad sitting in a wheelchair. The boys all sat down on the bags and settled in for the hour and a quarter trip to Carlisle. Everyone was chuffed they'd managed to get a seat of some sort and felt even more so because they'd done better than the poor buggers standing up squashed in the corridors. However, looking at the poor lad sat in his wheelchair who had been placed in the compartment by the guard all on his own, all of them felt a bit guilty that they could enjoy the day on their feet at the match and fiddle their way to a good seat and this poor lad couldn't do any of those things.

Don turned to Marc and whispered: 'Poor bugger. Imagine if that was you or me Marc? We're lucky you know eh.'

'Aye, we are Don.' And splitting a can from the plastic holding his last two cans of Guinness, he offered it to the disabled lad. 'Heh mate fancy a beer? You look thorsty?'

'Thanks, I'm clamming. There was no way I could get through that lot to a buffet. I was late for the train at the station too so never had a chance to eat,' said the wheelchair-bound young man taking the Guinness and cracking it open. He guzzled it all of it in swallow, squashed the can and threw it amongst the baggage. Don offered him another can and he took it gratefully.

'Here mate, take my pasty. Looks like you need it more than me,' said Jacko and he handed him the prize pasty he'd bought at the station buffet.

'Cheers,' the wheelchair boy said as he took the still warm pasty. 'I struggled to get to a buffet at the station.'

'Aye, must be difficult mate eh,' Jacko said, matter of factly.

Mackie sat brooding. Not known for his compassion to other human beings on the football pitch or nightclub, he had soft spot for the disadvantaged. He got up and walked over the short distance to the wheelchair and pushed it nearer the lads. Leaning down and giving his new found friend's back a slap he said: 'There mate, it's easier for you to talk. And we can hand you beer and bait eh.' And he gave him his last can of lager and a pork pie.

The lad supped the can pretty quickly and squashed it and threw it away like the last one. 'Cracking that,' he said wiping his lips and starting on his pie.

'Do you need a piss or anything mate?' Don asked.

'Nah, I'm all right at the moment. Don't fancy having to push through all that lot, it'll have to wait.'

'Aye, it'll be hell trying to get through them eh. Just give us a shout if you need us to help mate.'

The lad nodded nonchalantly, looked strangely at Don, half smiled and accepted a chocolate *Lion Bar* from Jacko.

Talk turned to the match. Marc stared at the blank walls of the baggage wagon. The train started to slow down as it approached Penrith. The lad in the wheelchair looked worried and said to his new found friends: 'I guess this is my stop.'

'Where's the bloody guard. He should be here by now to open the doors,' Mackie said, agitated, his green scary eyes blazing.

The wheelchair bound man said: 'Don't want a guard here mate. Last thing I want. I've got no ticket. I'll **** off now and try to get outta the door.'

Each one of the lads was about to say, '*Heh, don't do that we'll help*' when the boy leapt off his wheelchair, walked past the lads to the baggage room door and opened it into the packed corridor.

Mackie shouted at him, as the others just sat staring backwards and forwards at him and then the wheelchair. 'What the ****! We thought you were crippled, eh.'

The lad looked puzzled. 'I don't know why you thought that. I did what you did. Used the baggage room but when I came in there was this empty wheelchair so I sat in it. More comfy than you lot sat on the bags, eh.' And he shut the baggage door, squeezed past those in the carriage and jumped out of the open train door onto the platform.

The Everton lads looked at each other dumbstruck for a long time and then doubled up with laughter. Well, Mackie didn't, he repeatedly punched the mail bags all the way to Carlisle!

Meanwhile, Crazy Jim skipped along Penrith station pleased he'd eaten that *Lion Bar* – he'd been peckish. He strolled whistling to himself towards the station buffet bar, his favourite extendible cosh in his pocket. He pulled on his balaclava, took out the plastic gun and threw the doors open wide...

EPILOGUE
Black Magic Curses and Hope

Well, this book has been about the past - a magic carpet ride rolling through decades of cultural and technological change in the world that Aladdin, Niall Quinn and that bloody annoying blue Genie could never have dreamed of. Like Aladdin from his magic carpet we have seen *a whole new world* evolve from the time some of us, and even more of our fathers and grandfathers, watched Newcastle's 1956 FA Cup win and Sunderland's win in 1973. We have experienced a world of smart phones, the internet, space travel, social media, social isolation and VAR - yet never seen a Wembley win or a single Mackem in Madrid. However, even through the football's tragedies, I bet that these times have been the best years of your lives? A Paradise Lost forever. It will never be the same. You might want to remind yourselves how great these times outside of football were so I have left you all a historical and humorous narrative about the good times of growing up in my next book *Tin Baths, Hot Summers and Rock n' Roll*; a social history of when the world was young and we were happy. But now, as for the future, football will move on as will our lives, moving through an even faster pace of technological and social change. And for many of us, so will the relentless misery of following our team move inexorably on. However, for some obviously psychologically disturbed reason we will never give up.

'Whoever Till I Die', for all true supporters of all teams. I salute you all.

Well, obviously not in a mad March hare Di Canio salute way, but a suitable WOKE type one.

I have introduced you to the cast of Ali Baba and his forty thieves in these fables of many Arabian Nights. The moving finger having writ will have to move on. However, I can't leave you like that – miserable. There has to be a happy ending surely? Even though all of the actors, even with the magic carpet they were promised, and even Crazy Jim, could not scheme their way out of the misery of winning sod all.

Yet even now, as I end this rubaiyat, there is a glimmer of some HOPE.

Indeed, as I write, it is looking like some success is just around the corner for all of them. Well, maybe not for Mick and his Newcastle mate. Talk as I close this story of Saudi Princes and all that again may well happen but the human rights issues will not go away I fear. Nothing much seems to have changed with The Toon since I started writing this and I guess Mick's mate was correct...'Nobody lives that long'.

Sunderland have a new child owner who has a few billion quid in his trust fund as pocket money for the tuck shop so we can only speculate that he will invest in players and not in pineapple chunks. The disappointment of yet another playoff loss to Lincoln City and an empty stadium Wembley win was again a bitter sweet end to the season.

Let us hope for Manic Manc next year he can enjoy the transit van ride back up the M1, even with Ginger Gus farting all the way. Obviously, if we still endure Covid restrictions we will rely on Crazy Jim to scam the Club Wembley tickets yet again with the new Press Ticket con he told me about last night from his prison cell. I do hope so, because maybe the kids can sit next to Peter Reid and Chris Kamara again.

Exeter failed again. So Ben and his Dad continue in the relentless misery of the pursuit of what good is. And with Glasgow Rangers finally breaking Celtic's domination this resurrection of the blue and white side of Glasgow may well soften the heart of Harry the Hun and bring him to reconciliation with his green and white demons and finally a true forgiveness of his enemy...but I feel Bill Struth will turn in his grave if that ever happens! We can only Hope.

And Partick Thistle, well now only one division below Rangers and Celtic has to be a great hope for Denis. I look forward to eating a whole half roasted cabbage, large boiled spuds with beef gravy washed down with a bottle of Chassa de la Clyde in the Executive Suite again when they finally play one of the Old Firm. What more would one man want? I can't wait to go back!

Even Hartlepool won promotion back into the league yesterday much to the despair of another long suffering real football team, Torquay United.

So I pray that a happy future is ahead for us all. However, today as I was sending this manuscript off to the publisher, I had some shocking news which knocked my enthusiasm back. I hear from the psychiatric nurse in the secure wing that Manic Marc was rubbing his cursed black magic pot the other day and dreaming about that Champion's League Cup again. His daughter arrived as he was cutting bits off the newly grown hair on his bald head and burning them in the fire. Sorry, you may be wondering why? I must explain.

Many moons ago Marc and John found a sealed black porcelain pot on a beach in Singapore. It had funny Arabic writing on it. They both thought it might have contained some jewels or maybe, as it was near 9-11, possibly a bomb. Marc hoped it might have come from Arabia and contain a treasure map to find Niall Quinn's magic carpet ride. But of course, if you've read this book line by line, you'd know he was delirious. They were both clapping happily then and believed in widower's pensions, a good football team, magic Irish/Arabian carpets and rosy futures.

John took the pot to work. However, none of the local Indonesian, Malay, Indian or Chinese engineers could decipher it. So he took it to an Algerian piping engineer who read Arabic. He took one look, dropped the pot and ran out shouting:

'It's a black magic curse! Oh my, oh my, take it to the mosque quickly. It has to be prayed over by the Iman - only Allah can break it.'

John picked up the pot and stared at the Arabic writing closely and promptly threw it in the bin.

Back in the pub they laughed at the luck they had finding a curse and not treasure but thought nothing of it. However, many years later, after Marc lost his business, his money, his pub and nearly his life and John had lost his savings and suffered great tragedy in his family and then more horrors, David Moyes had come and gone and Danny Graham returned, they were sure it was the Black Magic Pot curse.

Manic Marc did what he was born to do, he got more manic as his luck disappeared and the league position of SAFC got worse. He started to study Arabic and ancient Indonesian black magic curses. Sadly, he began to pull out tufts of what hair he had left and burn them on a fire as he'd read on the internet that this was the only way to lift the curse. It didn't work. As you will have gathered, and Ginger Gus was always convinced, he may not be quite 'reet in the heed' of course.

When the hairless man received his diagnosis of doom from the doctor, John attempted to cheer him up by suggesting that when he died he'd make sure he'd have him burnt and he'd grind his ashes into a similar black magic pot in memory of the black pot curse. Selfishly, John hoped it might take the curse off him once his best mate had passed on to the Champion's league in the sky. The poor man thought this a good idea, but he had his own cunning plan, as he always had, and requested that John leave it on his mother-in-law's mantelpiece. He was terrified the curse would follow him to the afterlife and it might prefer to stay in a new pot and haunt her. But then he had a thought; 'John, I want you to take the pot with the ashes to St James and sprinkle them on there.'

John laughed. 'Aye, that'll put a curse on them Marc.'

He looked deadly serious. 'Bugger the curse! The next wind that comes along will blow the evil ashes into the buggers' eyes while they're watching the match and maybe blind the bastards.'

John chuckled but Manic Marc didn't. Some people are simply intractable – or mad. Instead of the blowing in the wind ploy, which relied far too much on the weather and chance, Marc agreed John should throw the pot off the Tyne Bridge as a physical eulogy in memory of him. He hoped it would ebb and flow with the tide past St James for an eternity, cursing them, like it had him - forever.

Now miraculously, his hair has grown back due to female hormone treatment for his cancer. This was a bonus for the demented man. But as usual the curse still prevailed and he believed the drugs were turning him into 'a lass'. He explained to John one day he was certain he was either 'turning gay or 'into a lass' because he had a small bumper collision with a man in a black and white shirt in a Tesco car park and he'd got out of the driver's seat without taking his axe this time. He'd apologised and they exchanged insurance details. It seems they chatted about the weather and the price of watching the match online and the state of each other's teams. Then in an act of almost incredible reconciliation he shook the man's hand and wished him all the best.

But the strangest, and most worrying side effect of the treatment, was that he was even starting to talk to their lass. You may say, this last is far too heavy a price to pay for his life saving treatment,

His loving daughter who has just given him a granddaughter, whom he insisted she call Charlie, after the legend man mountain Charlie Hurley, asked a perfectly sensible question of him as to why he was burning his hair.

'I'm trying to kill the curse pet. Ah've been studying Arabic and Indonesian black magic and it says borning my hair and chanting, *It's the hope I can't stand'* in Arabic might tak the black pot curse off John and me. Once that bastard curse has gone, we might finally win that trophy afor I die.'

And he threw more hair into the fire, got onto his knees, and bowed his head to the floor as if praying to Mecca.

He started chanting: 'إنه الأمل الذي لا أستطيع الوقوف عليه' He raised his body and head and looked at the fire and the raised his hands in the air. He bowed down placing his head on the fire rug. He chanted again the same mantra: 'إنه الأمل الذي لا أستطيع الوقوف عليه'

'Stop that dad. You are not going to die before we win something,' Charlie's mum said lovingly. She was used to comforting her constantly tormented father.

Still on his knees, he placed the pot on the fire hearth. He looked up at his daughter and with a voice full of the pathos only a Sunderland supporter could feel, he stuttered out: 'This pot has cursed John and me for eighteen years. And I've supported Sunderland for over sixty bloody years! Sometimes I wonder if I'm meant to suffer.'

190

He looked dolefully at his offspring who was gently patting what new grown hair he had left after immolating most of it .Then he uttered a final peroration: 'Mind you pet, sometimes I have a thowt that it would be nice to climb those steps to St Peter and finally get some rest - somewhere I can be certain there are none of them black and white bastards.'

His caring daughter understood his angst but she was also a realist and thought she'd bring him back to reality.

'But Dad, what if God supports Newcas...?'

She never completed that last word for the cursed man stopped her as he saw the terrible vision of a magpie-shirted St Peter at the pearly gates and his mouth dribbled and he screamed a long garbled exclamation; 'Ar......gh.'

Wounded to the heart, he rolled over on the carpet onto his back, overturning his lovely knitting basket - in his new found femininity he'd started knitting claar hammer red and white tank tops for his Cumbrian mates.

His mind was numb, cruelly stricken with the fact that this was the secret diabolical knowledge that the black pot carried all along - *God supports them bastards!*

He looked lovingly at his daughter and knew he was finished. The curse finally delivered.

I hear he has yet to speak again.

For sure the sad fate of Marc confirms it all:

Through the **Relentless Misery** of it all....

It's the Hope we can't stand

Disclaimer

If there are any Arabic speakers out there and this translation of 'It's the hope I can't stand', 'إنه الأمل الذي لا أستطيع الوقوف عليه', happens to be false and offends the Prophet, blessings be upon him, or the Holy Quran, it is purely co-incidental and unintentional. I'm sorry lads the writing looks like a doctor's prescription to me so I am relying on the translators in Google; if it's not accurate please reserve any dissent for them. I'm not in Salman Rushdie's financial literary league and can do without a bloody Fatwa the state I'm in with my back. And with the lads about to win the Champion's league that would be just my bloody luck.

Printed in Great Britain
by Amazon